SANDC

MW00889783

2023

Front Cover: Vermillion Flycatcher
Artist: Jon Sebba

SANDCUTTERS 2023 ANTHOLOGY

The Arizona State Poetry Society (ASPS) is a non-profit, all-volunteer organization founded in 1966 dedicated to the art of poetry and to the appreciation, writing, reading, and speaking of poetry. We promote poetry at the state and local levels and serve to unite poets in fellowship and understanding, while embracing diversity in skin color, gender identity, nationality, ethnicity, religion, socio-economics, language, different abilities, age, and neurodiversity. ASPS is a member of the National Federation of State Poetry Societies (NFSPS).

The Arizona State Poetry Society offers an annual journal, **Sandcutters**, published and copyrighted by the ASPS. We accept manuscripts from members *only* for the Member Contests, while the Annual Contest and Youth Contest are open to all poets, members and non-members of ASPS. Information on all contests can be found on our website at: https://azpoetry.net.

In the 1960s, the founding members of the Arizona State Poetry Society chose the title *Sandcutters* for this anthology to honor and poetically reflect Arizona's pioneer spirit. The early settlers were called "Sandcutters" because the wheels of their wagons and stagecoaches cut through the territory's desert sands with the objective to reach their promised land. Today, the membership of ASPS stands firmly upon a legacy of poets who perpetuated that unique spirit. They strive to continue the founders' poetic tradition as they make their own distinct marks in the sand, trusting those who will come after to carry on the society's longstanding commitment to poetry and community.

Thank you to ALL who submitted poems to our contests and congratulations to all the winners. We look forward to another great year of writing and reading poetry in 2024!

William Moody
Roadrunner

PRESIDENT'S MESSAGE

There is no other way to say it: the Arizona State Poetry Society is on fire! Exciting activities are in the plans, and membership growth is sizzling. Our Board of Directors is evolving to accommodate a roundhouse of innovative ideas, making ASPS one of the most active state poetry organizations in the nation. We just received an award for Special Achievement in Promotion from the National Federation of State Poetry Societies (NFSPS).

I want to begin by thanking some people who have graciously given their time and expertise to ASPS this year. Thanks to Jan Fuller, Johnny Chavez, and Renee Palting. Alan Perry is leaving his Program Director position to edit *RockPaperPoem* and will be sorely missed. Christy White, who has served ASPS in a myriad of roles since 1996, is now working as Outreach Chair to youth and adult poets. As Member Contest Chair, Dianne Brown delighted us with her animated emails. Allison Fraclose will take her place in 2024.

I attended the NFSPS convention in June, titled "Catch Poetry: Stage & Page," run side-by-side with the BlackBerryPeach National Poetry Slam, named for the surnames of the three people who started it. I cheered on 2023 AZ State Representative Ben Gardea (B-Jam) as he placed in the top 10 at the national competition. I asked B-Jam if he could help ASPS members stretch themselves to present more engaging stage performances of their poetry. He held October workshops in both Tempe and Tucson. At the ASPS **Annual Conference** January 19-21, 2024, volunteers from the workshops will give a presentation of their learning alongside SLAM poets. Our other headliners for the Conference? Sit down! We've got **Lauren Camp**, New Mexico's Poet Laureate; **Laura Tohe**, Poet Laureate for the Navajo Nation; and **Caleb Rainey**, "the Negro Poet," winner of SLAM competitions across the United States.

More workshops are in the lineup: an online generative workshop into the mirrors in our lives to explore **who we are, what it means to be a person, and how we perceive the world**; a generative workshop on forgiveness with Eleanor Kedney whom you met at last year's ASPS conference, another on the sonnet form by Western Colorado's poet laureate, and one connecting compassionate listening with an understanding of Other. B-Jam will be touring Arizona and holding SLAM competitions, looking for the next ASPS State Champion representative to send to the 2024 BlackberryPeach Nationals!

2024 looks like an even more dynamic year than 2023! I'm thrilled to be a part of ASPS with you.

Katie Sarah Zale
ASPS President

TABLE OF CONTENTS

President's Message ~ Katie Sarah Zale

MEMBER CONTEST WINNERS

ARIZONA YOUTH CONTEST WINNERS

ANNUAL CONTEST WINNERS

ASPS Member Poems

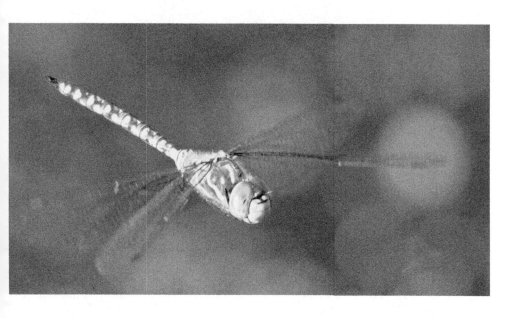

Jon Sebba
Dragonfly

FEATURED POET

Lauren Camp

Lauren Camp is a 2023 Academy of American Poets Laureate fellow and the author of seven books, most recently *An Eye in Each Square* (River River Books) and *Worn Smooth between Devourings* (NYQ Books). Her honors include a Dorset Prize and finalist citations for the Arab American Book Award, Housatonic Book Award and Adrienne Rich Award for Poetry. She is an emeritus fellow for Black Earth Institute and was Astronomer in Residence at Grand Canyon National Park. Her poems have been translated into Mandarin, Turkish, Spanish, French, and Arabic. She currently serves as Poet Laureate of New Mexico. She currently serves as Poet Laureate of New Mexico. She is also an emeritus fellow for Black Earth Institute and was Astronomer in Residence at Grand Canyon National Park. www.laurencamp.com.

Featured Poem   **Lauren Camp**

Stay Into

Not the absence of sky but the sudden
work of life: lance or ash, shovel,
notch or wince, I begin
inside myself to sing a prayer

for nourishment a feat
of the spirits I was taught one summer
at a wooden table, a knot
of bread, the euphony

of childhood I memorized
those unwrapped syllables rolling
immersion over years the words
have gone
I take to rhapsodic humming it was

never bounty
but simplicity
a time spun to habit ordinary
inclination a sort of fantasy
god I adored that childhood

those colors I made from my breathing
even the dimly, the stubborn farthest pitches
all this time I've kept
on the lip that ancient song map the divine
worn smooth between devourings.

Published in *Worn Smooth between Devourings* (NYQ Books, 2023)

FEATURED POET

Laura Tohe

Laura Tohe is Diné. She is Sleepy Rock people clan born for the Bitter Water people clan and is the daughter of a Navajo Code Talker. A librettist and an award-winning poet, she has written three books of poetry, edited two books, and wrote an oral history book on the Navajo Code Talkers. Her commissioned libretto, *Enemy Slayer, A Navajo Oratorio*, world premiered for the Phoenix Symphony and her latest libretto, *Nahasdzaan in the Glittering World* was performed in France in 2019 and 2021. Among her awards are the 2020 Academy of American Poetry Fellowship, 2019 American Indian Festival of Writers Award, and the Arizona Book Association's Glyph Award for Best Poetry. She is Professor Emerita with Distinction from Arizona State University and is the current Navajo Nation Poet Laureate.

My Eyes Are Small

An homage to the Grand Canyon

my eyes are small;

      they take only tiny licks at the walls of this canyon

my ears pick up my late brother's footsteps cracking on the Kaibab trail

my voice a whisper,

      a feather drifting on the wind

and yet my soul immense with the millennia of rocks and stars

rises,
      rises,
            rises,
                  rises

*First published as a recording by *ASU Now* (Arizona State University), 2019

Jon Sebba
Butterfly on Flower

JANUARY MEMBER CONTEST

Judged By

John Hilton

Indiana-based poet, Hinton's writing is inspired by human interactions and accompanying emotions of love, hate, indifference, passion. His words explore who we are, how we behave. Eloquent and gritty, his words reveal the joy and pain of our beautiful human existence.

Hinton also serves as President of the Poetry Society of Indiana. In this role, he works toward the goal of helping people discover and express their personal voice through poetry.

January Category I: Traditional Form
Henry A. Childers ~ Tucson, Arizona

The Nun

the nun at the table
was sitting up straight
rapping her knuckles
on the edge of the plate
face hard as wood
eyes still as stone
mouth firm in purpose
hands mostly bone
she was God's stout stick
His rod and His staff
and it was her mission
to stamp out the laugh
to throttle it in children
scorn it in the grown
and then confront the dying
with the seeds that they had sown
the priests could hear confession
but she'd have none of that
it's original sin and final
and that is simply that

January Category I: Traditional Form ~ A Homolinguistic Poem
Linda R. Payne ~ Ramsey, Minnesota

Winter Forest

inspired by Robert Frost's
Stopping by the Woods on a Snowy Evening

Who owns this forest? I perceive
he lives in town. I do believe
he'll never know I tarried here
and watched the snowflakes interweave.

My smallish mount must wonder why
we dallied here, no house nearby,
just icy pond and trees surround
us underneath the black night sky.

His bells make an impatient sound;
he stamps his hooves upon the ground.
A gentle sigh blows through the trees
as white confetti float around.

In peaceful shades of ebony
the woods entice with reveries,
but duty calls before my ease
but duty calls before my ease.

January Category I: Traditional Form ~ A Miltonic Sonnet
Laura Rodley ~ Shelburne Falls, Massachusetts

Unfurled

Green acorns fall holding their caps, asleep
with the DNA of oaks that they keep
even when buried deep by a squirrel
who forgets one or two with his toil,
but the seed remembers when spring returns;
a little rain, a little sun, the burn
of a new leaf reaching through, roof of sky
so high overhead, everything new, fly
-ing robins newly home, returned, so young
the oak's new leaves mirror their short wings flung
open soaring on eddies of air, the sky's
ocean: all this from the small seed thrown by
the tall oak standing on the path I walk
daily, hundreds of acorns, and they talk.

January Category II: Free Verse
Dianne Brown ~ Wellton, Arizona

Small Towns - Selected Memories

Have you ever noticed
small towns walk more slowly
speak more softly
listen to country music
and old time
Rock 'n' Roll

The commerce
of living is filled
with smiles
on a first-name basis
and *how-do-you-dos*

Backyards filled
with kids playing
Gardens planted
growing in the
summer heat

Evenings see folks
on porches in swings
background laughter
and fireflies
fill the air

Sunday picnics
spread under shade trees
fried chicken
watermelon
and lemonade

Have you ever noticed
small town people
enjoy their dogs
root for the home team
fill life to the brim

January Category II: Free Verse
Charles Firmage ~ Eloy, Arizona

Crumbs

Otis Redding's song, "Sittin' on the dock
of the bay ... wastin' time," keeps running
through my mind, but I'm sitting
on this park bench feeding pigeons,
instead of watching gulls diving
into the waves. Some say if I didn't feed 'em,
they'd go away, make the city cleaner,
a bit greener, but it's peaceful here.
Noah sent out a dove that came back
with an olive branch. Actually, pigeons
are rock doves, brought first
to Nova Scotia in the early 1600s by the
French. Do pigeons promote peace?
Chicago, San Francisco, and so many
other big cities've seen crime escalate,
is it too late to hope? But who knows
if the birds don't help to keep the violence
from boiling over? The Sermon on the Mount
tells of the birds not reaping nor sowing,
but God feeds 'em, maybe He gave that job
to me. I pick up bread crumbs from
the soup kitchens and leave them for the
sparrows outside my window at the veterans
home. The birds don't care it it's
gluten-free, low-cal, or if it has raisins.
Now the country's tearing down statues,
where will all the pigeons go to roost?
I hear well-dressed folks strolling
past my bench, discussing what my political
beliefs might be, if I'm blue. If I'm red.
I just say, red, white, and blue, and throw
more crumbs on the grass.

January Category II: Free Verse
Mary Heyborne ~ Sedona, Arizona

Threadbare Night Shirt and New Years Eve

Finally sorting through your clothing,
I clung to your well-worn night shirt,
held it tightly to my face
and breathed—
and breathed.

I began wearing it for comfort
but soon felt it falling apart
and returned it to its private drawer.

Years later, I don it on special nights
to feel you nestling me.
Oversized, it totally cocoons me
and—though threadbare now—
wraps me in your remembered warmth.

It's New Years Eve,
and I approach the night shirt drawer.

Annette Gagliardi ~ Minneapolis, Minnesota

Candles Everywhere

At the corner where eternity prunes
time, saffron-yellow flames.

Candles placed around the room
draw light from surfaces,

twirl like mariachi dancers,
twinkle like fireworks.

Light reflects off mirrored surfaces,
softens wood, shimmers ceramic,

exposes shadowed seconds,
revealing the endlessness of time.

Fire creates silhouettes of blaze-faced
virgins, draws light and shadow on the

features of friends, creating hollow
saints and gilded sinners

with highlighted cheeks and hair.
Ignited light skims over everyone's skin,

pulling glow from within, building a fire
caught until we burn our brains

with a thousand, whispered moments. Candles
gutter while night pools moistly at our feet.

Still Water
   after Wendell Berry

Feeling blue this morning,
I pause at the pond's edge
to read Berry's poem
about going *where the wood drake*
rests in his beauty on the water.

I look up from my reading,
and there before me
that elegant creature,
that rare gift,
glides serenely.

In the stillness of wonder,
morning lifting into midday around me,
the wild things unmoved by my awe,
I know, in the fullness of a breath,
the balm of nature's grace.

The references in this poem are to *The Peace of Wild Things*, by Wendell
Berry

January Category III: Waves of Gratitude
Brenda Wildrick ~ Fort Morgan, Colorado

I Have Met Gratitude

on Garfield Street in Loveland
where Grandpa worked the garden
with railroad tracks behind him and Grandma
hung clothes and sheets on the clothesline
with clothespins in her mouth

and children hid Easter eggs in the laps of trees
and in holes in the fence made of cement blocks
and stood in awe of trains and waved to the man
in the window of the old red caboose

where Grandma bought gifts at after-Christmas
sales when K-mart was bran new and she'd
have them wrapped by April and by Christmas
she was as surprised as anyone
to see what she had given

where we all waded through scattered
wrapping paper on Christmas morning
and shared huge quantities of homemade
food, and whispered secrets in the dark
because family wasn't perfect

where Grandpa would sit in a wicker
rocking chair watching TV turned up loud,
smiling and nodding, pretending to hear
what the children said, and we'd ask
about his one black fingernail, the result
of some long ago hammer injury

So many cousins and make-believe play
We were cops and robbers, moms
and babies, spies and counterspies,
shop keepers and customers

Gratitude was childhood with Grandma
in an apron and Grandpa in overalls
and Sunday mornings when they and we
dressed up special

Kim Sosin
Egret Flying

MARCH MEMBER CONTEST

Judged By

Sharon Skinner

Sharon Skinner holds a GPC, a BA in English, an MA in Creative Writing and is a Certified Book Coach and freelance editor, whose goal is to help writers weave their words into stories that shine. She mainly writes fantasy, science fiction, paranormal, and the occasional steampunk, for audiences of all ages. But her roots lie in poetry. Her heart was smitten by verse when, in elementary school, her mother handed her a book titled, *100 Best Loved Poems*. Skinner is an active member of Society of Children's Book Writers and Illustrators (SCBWI) and serves as the Regional Advisor for SCBWI AZ. Her Young Adult and Middle-Grade novels tend to explore complex relationships, particularly those between mothers and daughters. She also served aboard the USS Jason, the first US Navy vessel to take women to sea (WestPac cruise). But that's another story. To learn more, visit sharonskinner.com or bookcoachingbysharon.com

March Category I: Traditional Form – Shape Poem
Lorraine Jeffery ~ Orem, Utah

Anything Will Do

-- Silence raises
                its hooded
                        head. Pungi
                                and
                                    swaying
                            will not
                        be
                        enough.
                        Bury
                it *with*
            raucous
        lyrics,
    with
        clicking
            heels,
                honking
                        horns,
                            strident
                                siren
                                    with
                                        moaning
                                        wind,
                                            grinding
                                        mower's
                                guttural growl.
                        Anything
                    will do.
                Else
            it will
        slither
grassward,
    creep
        under
            doors
                    and
                        strike
                            embedding toxic introspection.

If Some Grim Hawk

were not stooping over me,
wild music shrieking through black
pinions spread to cover me,
talons kissing my bruised back –

if Time were not a swift hound
belling joy and keeping close
through the scrub of words I've found
and passed, when I'm losing hope

and breath – then I might love dreams,
fall into the empty dark
without tears or coward's screams
and rise, a shining phoenix spark.

But Death loves this black pursuit
and hovers over every dream.
Nightmare is the bitter fruit
of tasting my mortality.

March Category 1: Traditional Form – Haiku

Ann Penton ~ Green Valley, Arizona

multiple listings~
not all perfect verticals
these Ponderosas

March Category II: Free Verse
Tina Durham ~ Hereford, Arizona

Feeling Blue

Snow blowing off a juniper,
flakes kissing your cheek,
a polychrome popsicle plucked from the eaves
and glistening in your glove.

Next day, rain plopping off the roof, pouring
over a glazed indigo planter.
A white rose sucking drenched, black soil.

The scent of pine needles
after the sun comes out.
The wings of a dragonfly
hovering over pink fireweed.

March Category II: Free Verse
Lorraine Jeffery ~ Orem, Utah

Blind Amanda and His Eyes

This tall man, A. P. Decuis' with the whitest skin,
        came and promised. You
dug clams, scooped mussels, baked camas root
        and smoked cod, before
your beautiful Julia, was born, while

your teeth cracked on acorns, and
        your eyes squinted cobwebs
in twilight. Treaty
        with the Alsea sub-agency. All
        not related to whites must
        go. He promised. When
you ask, he doesn't answer. You
        can't see his eyes. What
about Julia? *She*
        is mine. With soldiers,

and other Coos, you trek
ninety miles up the coast to Alsea. Cape

Perpetua stands in the way. *High*
        says the woman ahead of you. Your moccasin
soles grow holes up the narrow trails.
        Fir needles scrape,
        while your feet navigate roots
        and sharp stones. *Big*
drop, says the woman. *Hold*
        onto my shoulder. Salt

water wind whips the hair across your face. *Soon,*
        mutters a soldier. *Your footprints*
        bloody the trail, murmurs
        the man behind you. Brown eyes

follow. Weathered
        hands reach to guide. You whisper
        Julia.

March Category II: Free Verse
Ann Penton ~ Green Valley, Arizona

Walking In Her Shoes

Back then, Mom,
I got lost in the mundane mud,
struggling, overwhelmed,
slogging around turf too murky
and hurdles too many.

If only I could have navigated
differently and narrowed my focus
to just two clear choices:
>   *Did I want to be*
>   *a grey pebble in your shoe,*
>   *or a blue-green soft-gel insert?*
>   my next step would have been
>   so obvious.

>   Back then, Mom,
>   I didn't have the maps I do now.
>   *I'm sorry.*

The Language Of Faith

In Spring I have faith in the brazen splay
of Palo Verde blossoms and the bee's sweet addiction.

When I walk past a school yard and realize myself;
an older woman walking past a school yard, I have faith
in young voices pitched volley-ball high over a fence.

I climb the sheer side of this mountain, wade through
cold crossings up to my knees and if I meet another hiker,
I know he too has faith in the mountain and the trail.

Here on the desert, a dun-colored wren beaks her young
a breakfast of black beetle. I have faith in black beetle
and a sudden death taken up to give life.

The dead do not visit. Shadows of angels do not fall
across our rooftops even as they are honored in bas relief
carved in stone. Could it be they have no faith in us?

One evening in rural Maine, I saw my father hand his wife
a basket of strawberries, dripping with hose water.
His boots left black clods of earth
across her fresh-scrubbed kitchen floor
but she raised her smile to his and kissed him.
                    And I had faith in love.

For me it all begins when you say, Good Morning
and I find faith in eggs over easy, black coffee and devotion.
The day opens, closes like valves of the heart.
Silence says what it always says,"I speak beyond words".

When they told us your condition was terminal,
I found faith in one more day, one more hour.

There is a story about you and me,
I hear the coyote call it out through a hole in the sky.

Our story is the salty, wet earth of our bodies
and our faith in one another.
                    It is a short story but true.

Lorraine Jeffery ~ Orem, Utah

Weaving Guatemala's Colors

Weaving Guatemala's Colors
Needles in the compass -
your world, unlike mine, faces east
but the color is red, not sunrise yellow.

Father Sky, *white* defines the north,
Mother Earth, *yellow* the south.
Black for the west,
for the moon and death?
Did your enemies come from the west?

And beyond the compass,
you weave the *blue* of religion
and life-giving water from
Great Mother Ceiba in your
carvings, dances, pottery.

Stories and patterns pass
from mother to daughter
while you kneel to weave,
heavy ropes behind your back—
your loom in front.
Lean back to tighten,
lean forward to loosen,
weaving blankets, shawls
and your ubiquitous huipiles.*

Leaning,
you adjusted your looms
and your life to grief, wars,
famines and joy.

After years of brutal civil war,
you make worry dolls
but also blankets and huipiles,
with images of
shedding snakes
and quetzal birds.
Hope in a multicolored
jaguar rebirth.

*Huipiles - one piece of fabric folded end to end, then sewed up the straight
sides but leaving openings near the top for arms and head.*

March Category III: Propagating Beauty
Gurupreet K. Khalsa ~ Mobile, Alabama

Transcending Gravity

If cracked promises
fragment your shell of safety,
float as dandelion fluff
to alight in new, smooth soil.

If unfulfilled expectations
suck you into bottomless black maw,
become a peregrine falcon,
fly yourself to sunny Louisiana.

If quicksand doubt
suffocates resolve, smothers hope,
lift away like a luna moth,
drift on soft air currents.

If the unliftable boulder of endings
glues you to earth,
dissolve into particulate mist,
drift as fog among the trees.

If you are fixed in fire
stirred from glowing embers of despair,
become smoke curling
into cirrus clouds of sunrise.

Jon Sebba
Turtles

MAY MEMBER CONTEST

Judged By

Tiffany Brenneman

Tiffany Brenneman holds an MFA from Minnesota State University in Mankato and works in the Scholarly Commons at the University of Illinois. Her poems have appeared in *Cream City Review*, *Sugar House Review*, *After Hours,* and *Write City Magazine.*

May Category I: Traditional Form - Quatrain
Betty Jo Middleton ~ Alexandria, Virginia

Solitaire

Far above the sleeping earth
a single star is in the sky.
You lie tonight in another's arms
and alone as that star am I.

May Category I: Traditional Form - Haiku

Ann Penton ~ Green Valley, Arizona

this dead-end's
big garage sale lures them in~
catch and release

Keening Wall

Beside the tall pines
the wind keens, takes up my cries,
and keeps going through the harps
of trees bent sideways,
pine cones clunking down that
chipmunks later salvage for dinner.
The keening pines and maples
know their job well;
they've done it for generations,
long before my arrival, scything
the wind, pine needles dropping,
breaking open the first
maroon buds of the maples.
They check my pulse through
the moisture in the winds,
measure my heartbeat
against their lips.
Who will breathe for them,
who will breathe for my father
when oxygen no longer sustains him?

A True Cairn

I know what appears to be solid
is also constructed of space
and a form of liquidity, although
I can not say what that is.

Like a worm hole detected by an absence
either a way in or, maybe a way out.

No clear markings.
The cairn at the cove's inlet.
Disturbed ground, like a promise, at the foot of the black oak.
A tongue of, *what is that*, sticking up from the mud.

Somehow we fall forward anyway
step by step, holding hands, or not, and later
we walk out into the stars as fresh
as the first pure cry we hollered.

Here, we molt among murmuring sorrows
we refine, until our fragile solids are whisked
and unsorted into an absence
whose liquids found the long way out.

And there is nothing
nothing more to be known
or imagined so perfectly.

May Category II: Free Verse
Laura Rodley ~ Shelburne Falls, Massachusetts

Dairy Farming

A back is worth a million dollars;
is a herd worth a back,
milking for 60 years,
holding the hand of time?
Who drinks this cup of milk,
who bakes bread with its moisture?
All of you, all of you.

Soon the price will be too
high to afford, one back,
two backs, the herd
salvaged, but not the backs,
the herd sold, the hand
of time let go.

the Yaqui word for bird is wiilkit

> *so words, as weak as birds, survive because*
> *they move collectively and restlessly,*
> *as if under siege-* Fanny Howe

Phainopepla
from the Greek
when Isis
Unlocatable and Hidden
held her veil
that no one could lift
    to see the nature of
    to bring to light

struggles in the hand
of its captor
    in wooded California

being banded on its little foot
for the good of the flock (science)
and enlightenment
to track its travels
    where it eats mistletoe
    where it breeds -twice

in *bewilderment*
in quick mimicry
it reveals where it has been
it speaks in Arizona desert bird
    verdin   cactus wren
    quail and flicker
    finches and the wings of a mourning dove
    taking flight

then
small black bird
pejaro pequeno
in distress
    mimicks red-tailed hawk
    incorporeal raptor

May Category III: Being Underwater
Ann Penton ~ Green Valley, Arizona

Undercurrents

It was only one long summer—
away from home when I was thirteen.
Without trying I must have memorized
the distinct aroma of that gas-oil mix
Uncle Frank's little boat used as fuel
for its 5-horse motor, propelling me
forward, with unseen blades spinning
beneath the surface.

All it takes now (decades later)
is one tiny airborne tendril wafting
my way near some boat dock.
Just one whiff transports me back
by invisible forces over many miles—
an ever-curious girl on 9-Mile Creek,
with bag lunch packed and stowed,
setting off on another solo journey
among overhanging willows,
great blue herons, snowy egrets,
and no cares.

A Widow's Carpe Diem

A chorus of mourners,
last night's Nor'easter howling,
rain beating and rattling the old windows
of her guest room. I imagined my surroundings
no match for the churning ocean. Buildings do collapse
and my friend and I might be washed out to sea.
All night I cowered in my room beneath blankets.

Next morning nature's tantrum over, we gazed
at a tableau of ocean stillness under a blue bowl
of sky. We sipped tea, our shoulders touching.
She had slept well. With arms folded across
a chest flattened by cancer, she spoke
of navigating her way back without him:
Raised my window last night
as my Larry would
to hear the surf pounding!

She and I link arms, walk the beach.
It is terribly cold and I nuzzle into her
for warmth and courage.
She presses forward into the wind.

May Category III: Being Underwater
Brenda Wildrick ~ Fort Morgan, Colorado

Holding Our Breath

I drifted back in time at least 50 years.
And I was in her dreams. I saw her
wandering in a school hallway.
She couldn't read the numbers above
the doors because of the thick gray fog.
She didn't find what she was looking for,
because, even when she did enter one
of the rooms, a classroom full of strangers
stared blankly back at her.

In the hallway, holes appeared
in the floor and, as she struggled to avoid
falling into one of them, they grew larger
and larger until the non-hole parts of the floor
were so thin, it seemed inevitable that she
would fall in.

Then suddenly she was at the bottom of a pool,
holding her breath, struggling to swim to the top.
But each time she thought she had arrived and
could finally take a breath, there was more water.
She kept gasping for air, sure she would drown.

I tried to speak to her after the pool had
become a car. She was trying to drive from the
passenger side. She was scared, feeling out of
control, trying to navigate through heavy traffic.
I whispered to her, and she seemed to hear me.

"It will be okay, child," I said.
"You won't always feel like this."

Kim Sosin
Eagle

JULY MEMBER CONTEST

Judged By

Marianne Botos

A desert rat, Marianne lives in historic central Phoenix with her sweetheart and animal menagerie on their urban farm. She achieved her BA in journalism and MFA in poetry at Arizona State University. Among her honors and fellowship awards is an Arizona Commission on the Arts Fellowship/Creative Writing. Marianne's poetry has been widely published in journals and magazines, art exhibits, and even once in a tree. She teaches creative writing and literature at Paradise Valley Community College.

July Category I: Traditional Form
Charles Firmage ~ Eloy, Arizona

She Rocks the Cradle

She rereads letters Dan sent from Iraq. She
rocks little Ricky as she sings.
The times his daddy's been gone; the
cradle stands still as Pam puts away Dan's things.

Rocks little Ricky as she sings;
he might be walking before Dan gets home.
Pam sings 'bout sailing a boat, having wings
to fly them above the sea, above the foam.

The times his daddy's been gone; the
chance Dan'll miss his son's first steps.
If only she could fly, the sea
wouldn't be a wall …. She dreams of Dan's steps.

Cradle stands still as Pam puts away Dan's things,
she kept them out, hoping he'd soon be back.
Pam sorts through the mail the postman brings,
hoping for Dan's letter from Iraq,
she rocks the cradle.

July Category I: Traditional Form – Pantoum
Lydia Gates ~ Flagstaff, Arizona

We All Bleed

I was in love with a girl,
the softest apology of a woman—
tender in the way veal is:
kept gentle and compliant and guilty.

Every woman gives the softest apologies,
says, "Sorry," if she breathes too harshly,
only knows to be gentle and compliant and guilty
weighed down by original sin inherited.

She said, "Sorry." Her breath was a whisper when
I kissed the word right out of her mouth.
It tasted like original sin inherited,
so, I ripped that page from the bible out.

I kissed the prayers right off her lips,
the whispered repentance of her doubt.
So, I ripped a page from the dictionary
and crossed the word "sorry" out.

She doubted she could repent for this:
a transgression so sapphic it burned,
but I crossed my heart and loved her,
even caged and closeted we yearned.

A transgression so sapphic went up in smoke,
tender as veal just before the slaughter—
caged and closeted and kept, she yearned
calf, knife, sacrifice, a girl in love with a girl.

July Category I: Traditional Form - Envelope Quintet
Ann Penton ~ Green Valley, Arizona

"Envelope Quintet" – this one with rhyme form ABBBA is a type of "Quintain" Poem

Mapmaker's Dilemma

Shore line—
to pin down for maps
with all those tongue laps,
waves, white caps—
ever shifting, hard to define.

July Category II: Free Verse
Karen Admussen ~ Tucson, Arizona

powered by nature

sacred datura
dries into a miniature
desert machine, a crane
of Tinker Toy branches with
spiked seed pods resembling
industrial clamshell buckets
waiting to release tiny
hard black seeds
at the appointed
time

July Category II: Free Verse
Tina Durham ~ Hereford, Arizona

6:37

No one else is up.
Five books are stacked on the couch beside her,
poetry magazines are scattered across the floor.
She's feeling words rise in her, listening carefully
the way she listens to water
gurgling up from the pump.
It struggles slowly through rusty pipes.

She doesn't hear me walk into the kitchen
until I start the coffee.
There are white flakes in the pot.
We need new plumbing, but she won't move.
She likes the vines on the east side of the house –
moonflowers, nacreous trumpets
that call in the night.

She's heard me now and dropped her notepad.
Bare feet whisper across floorboards.
With a silver tabby draped over her shoulder,
she kisses me.
A moonflower is in her hair.

July Category II – Free Verse
Nan Rubin ~ Tucson, Arizona

Breakfast Prep and Prayers

Silently, I say a prayer *may you be well.*
Chop oranges, banana, arrange a cornucopia
of oatmeal fixings. *May you find safety.*
Set out boiled eggs, juice, tray of sweets and coffee.
Today, may kindness find you.

Breakfast for a moving column
of homeless women, layered
in what's readily worn,
stuffed in a backpack,
pulled along in a suitcase
tired and battered as its owner.
Sometimes a small dog
tucked under an arm
or led on a leash - two
heart beats grown attuned
for safety and solace.

They reach across the counter
for breakfast. Some with grime
in knuckles, under nails; others,
multiple rings on fingers,
chipped nail polish. Some bold,
pointing, *Give me this!* Others,
curled into shyness
when offered seconds.

They wander in
from beneath bridges,
encampments, a beat up car.
Most a portrait of
wariness, weariness
around eyes and mouth
shuffle and slope
of shoulders.
Wherever they sleep
never   safe   enough.

B24 Liberator

Confusion clung like heavy metal wings
not uplifting but dragging me to the ground.
I meandered around downtown window shopping
stopping at an antique store something catching
my attention like a random thought.
A kit for building a model airplane
a B24 Liberator.

Was it coincidence that my father flew a Liberator
in World War II? He is now stuck in a wheelchair
wanting most of all to go outside and ride in a car
my own confinement more intangible
but perhaps when mentally entrapped
a better solution to dissecting a problem
is putting it together piece by piece
and so I bought the model airplane kit.

Inside the box were hundreds of tiny plastic parts
and dozens of pages of instructions requiring
tweezers, magnifying glass, gorilla glue,
paints in a variety of greens, grays and browns
camouflage drab to hide from the enemy
gray belly indistinguishable from a wintry sky
olive green top blending with the fields below.
Only at altitude could his comrades distinguish
my father's N on the tail of the Naughty Nan.

Dad and I drove west into the sunset one evening
brilliant colors diving and weaving
orange, pink, red trapped in a huge cloud
itself a mix of cirrus, stratus, cumulus,
cumulonimbus culminating in a winter storm.

A real B24 has no forgiveness
slammed together in factories blown apart in sky
carrying men brave enough to climb aboard and roar
across the frigid English Channel
through a forest of German flak clinging
to the singing wings of companion planes and I
am an old lady building a model airplane.
It is obvious that my thinking is way too small
and liberation oh so frightening.

July Category III – Patriotic Memories
Gene Gant ~ Sun City, Arizona

Omaha Beach

The ocean seems to be holding us back
Knowing death lies in wait on the beaches

Then a sudden swell seems to throw us ahead
Into that hell that awaits us

There is no cover – there is nowhere to hide
From the hail of lead raining down

I hear cries of anguish and shouts of despair
From the wounded and dying around me

And yet – like a madman I race to the cliffs
And wonder – why death hasn't found me

That was decades ago – but I still recall
As though it was yesterday

That fateful morning – on Omaha beach
When so many died – in so short a time

On D-day, I sit – while some self-righteous twit
Makes a speech – to impress his peers

While I gaze at the ghosts – that he'll never see
On the beaches of Normandy

July Category III: Patriotic Memories
Brenda Wildrick ~ Fort Morgan, Colorado

Gazing into the Darkening Sky

I remember 4th of July
corn knee-high in the fields,
heavenly aroma of hamburgers
sizzling on the grill,
sticky watermelon juice
dripping from smiles, running
down small chins.

In those years we all watched the same news
and forgot about politics
as soon as elections were over.
I remember sitting on an old blanket,
or the hood of a sturdy car, gazing up
into the darkening sky. Anticipating.

I remember whispering a prayer of gratitude
for peace, prosperity, and freedom,
with underlying acknowledgment –
there is no guarantee we will enjoy
these privileges forever.

I remember red, white, and blue
Flags flying – too often these days at half-mast
Flags painted – enormous on sides of barns
Flags as weapons – breaking windows,
beating police officers.

Patriotism is fighting, is defending.
But in the 2020's, the enemy is within.
We are destroying ourselves
as we attack each other.
We have confused our own language.
We abandon the tower of babel and scatter.

Is dividing the answer?
Blue here, Red there
Slash apart states. Slash apart families.

I imagine another option.
Gathering scattered words, sorting,
we find the kind words, piece them together.
We create a new common language.

Kim Sosin
Great Horned Owl

SEPTEMBER MEMBER CONTEST

Judged By

Mary Ann Westbrook

Mary Ann originally haled from upstate New York. When her husband retired, they bought a travel trailer, sold the house and roamed the country for seven years. They spent several winters in the Arizona deserts which they came to love. They ended up settling on the east coast of Florida near Daytona Beach and are four houses from the Atlantic Ocean and ten houses from the intracoastal waterway. Needless to say, they love it there!

Mary Ann is the current President of Tomoka Poets Society of Ormond Beach, and past Secretary/past President of Florida State Poets. She is also current Vice President of Creative Happiness Institute that supports all of the Arts but especially poetry. And to cap it off she is Head Usher at the Peabody Auditorium, which is a live performance theater.

Sally Boyington ~ Knoxville, Tennessee

century plant

spiraling leaves like petals on a rose
set in a Fibonacci sequence
from tender center each leaf grows

long and graceful arching form
armed at tip with piercing dagger
each edge lined with clawing thorns

carefully blended artist's palette
in watercolor blue-green hues
embossed with arcs where overlapped

not a sentinel growing alone
but a colonizer preparing the ground
for pups it puts out when fully grown

heart fattened by the desert sun
it sends up one thick flower stalk
and blooms in glorious death hard-won

leaves and clouds stir
one elk strolls by
~silent movie

The House

A tin house with no roof to catch the rain,
no windows packed with snow at winter time,
no moonlight on the porch
that is not there,
no flowers blooming in
summer sunshine,
just a plain house put there
for all to see
and fill with dreams of life lived wishfully ...
the home-grown moment,
a garden-to-be
and small garage to store our yesterdays
but far from what you called reality—
my wished-for world where we live happily.

Wedding Bells

Something borrowed, something new,
blue flowers in October arranged
with white ribbons on the altar
of your leaving, your wedding
your leaving, your devotion,
turning the turnstile of his heart.
Watch you slip your hand in his,
watch the rings thrust promises
like confetti into their air,
your gown carried by three
bridesmaids, glowing with youth,
love. Give you away, your father will,
but so will I, and
you won't sleep in our house anymore,
leave your clothes or call
saying, "I'm here if you need me;"
I'll be feeling something old, something blue.

September Category II: Free Verse
Stuart Watkins – Tucson, Arizona

4th Avenue, Anchorage, Alaska

Dark stale beer
revibrating rhythms of din
that blot out misery
through warm beer suds
and touching bodies
and dreams of places
brighter and bolder
anywhere other
than the Montana Club
But here I am
Anchorage, Alaska
and I am so down
bum a beer, bum a kiss
bum a warm embrace
and stumble home
but where is home
there is no home but this
maybe the Elbow Room
or the Scandinavian Club
or the Adult Book Store
but somehow through the haze
friendships since past come through
into my mind of booze
and tears break down the restrain
of this broken bum of a man
and my stubble is wet again
from the dribble on my chin

September Category II: Free Verse
Brenda Wildrick ~ Fort Morgan, Colorado

Pain is a Heavy Backpack

His pain he carried with him
in a heavy dark backpack,
stuffed full of his laptop,
books, and various possessions
given to him by people
who had long ago distanced
themselves from him.

He wore too much clothing
in warm weather.
When he went out walking,
he never appeared light
and unencumbered.

Even during times he had a home,
he couldn't set his pain down,
leave it in a room.
He could never trust anyone
with the pain he packed away,
so he carried it with him
everywhere he went.

No Closer

Some say we can't keep secrets in small towns,
but I have plenty, like when I was young
I wanted to be a disc-jockey or
a writer, but who'd understand, so I
ended up in my old man's agency
insuring autos, homes, and lives, husbands
and wives coming in to pay premiums,
while I secretly wanted to be on
the road with Jack Kerouac, far away
from the Fond-du-Lac road, the boulevard
where my office stood, where my journey of
a thousand miles should have begun. Yes, I'm
secretly in love with Annie at the
local library, who's always stamping
books, but when she looks up at me, I'm no
closer to knowing her. I wonder if
she yearns to be free from care, riding on
a motorcycle with the wind in her
hair or walking on the beach and watching
the waves rolling in, but Wisconsin's far
away from California. So I check
books out by Emily Dickinson and
Shakespeare just to be near her, but I'm still
secretly reading books by Malcolm X
and poems by John Lennon. The next time
I'm at her desk, she asks me how I liked
Robert Frost's poems. I long to tell her
I'd like to take those glasses off, the ones
on the chain around her neck, and to …, but she'd
only "shush" me and say, "Quiet, please." Like
Marian the librarian in, "The
Music Man," and go on stamping the due
dates at the back of the books. Once she came
into the agency for a quote on
her car, but I wasn't in. That's close as
she got to my world. She asked me how I liked
Elizabeth Barret Browning's poems
I returned. I started to say, "You must
know how I love you, let me tell you the
ways," but I only smiled as I answered,
"I liked them fine."

Ann Penton ~ Green Valley, Arizona

Elegy for Steve

[after news learned late about my student who died from complications of HIV acquired from a youthful blood transfusion]

I remember you sat high in the back row
somehow separate in the college classroom
even on days when another student sat near you.
You were a tousled blond,
yet becoming a yellow-grey candle
melting slowly from long heat
rather than from any one recent flame.

A tired puppy who couldn't quite stay awake—
hints of sparkle in the eye or a wag of the tail
but so limp after circling and circling
and falling into rest.

You were distant in the way of soldiers,
still living, but having seen too much,
with invisible wounds folks could sense but not see.
You were not just in the last row
but somehow already above   outside   elsewhere.

Once a playful otter up close,
you were sliding away from us
after a long run—but not too long.
You were only twenty-one.

If only I –or any of us at the college—
had been allowed to peek into your world
before seeing the obituary, attending the funeral,
reading newspaper stories.
If only we could have understood and
appreciated why you chose to keep coming to classes.
If only we knew of your fears.

If only we knew of you
and your antics in a clown-suit
they say brightened earlier summers
at camp with the other kids.

That's how I'll remember you now.

September Category III: The Secret He/She Keeps
CChristy White ~ Phoenix, Arizona

Wicked Secrets *(In Two Voices)*

Tell her

          Tell him

your secret   your secret
the one

          you keep
hidden   hidden
from everyone

          from everyone

she would

          he would
hate you   hate you
if she

          if he
knew   knew

Tell   Tell
before someone else

          because someone else

in conversation

          on the phone

over coffee

          forgetting it is a secret
will speak   will speak
and then

          it's over

just like that
soft caresses

          sweet kisses
gone   gone

Tell her

          Tell him
your secret   your secret

Patricia Fremont Smith
Gambel's Quail

2023 Arizona Youth Poetry Contest

The Arizona State Poetry Society offered its first ever state-wide youth poetry contest in Arizona!

With the assistance of the Arizona Department of Education, ASPS publicized this contest to all public schools in Arizona, as well as many private schools and home schools.

Under the leadership of ASPS Outreach Chairperson, Christy White, we received over 1,000 submissions in three separate categories:

Grades 1-4
Grades 5-8
Graces 9-12

Prize Awards

Grades 1-4	Grades 5-8	Grades 9-12
First Place ~ $30	First Place ~ $35	First Place ~ $50
Second Place ~ $20	Second Place ~ $25	Second Place ~ $30
Third Place ~ $10	Third Place ~ $15	Third Place ~ $20

We thank the Arizona Department of Education for helping us publicize this contest, to the many educators who helped promote the contest in their schools, Christy White for her hard work in running the Contest, and the judges for their discernment.

We look forward to offering the contest each year. We recognize that youth are the future of our Society and we look forward to encouraging all students to express themselves through poetry.

ARIZONA STATE YOUTH CONTEST
Grades 1-4

Judged By

Resa Ferreira

Resa to many, Gramma to two, and Beloved to one. Resa Ferreira loves the sounding of words on paper, through breath and in all visual media. She'll be weaving those sounds until death comes to walk her over the bridge to the next island. Resa studied Theatre Arts at Wells College, and is a storyteller, poet, and writer. She lives in Connecticut with her husband, Steve. They both present workshops on story, healing, and personal myths, and have presented at a number of venues over the years. https://spiritsound.weebly.com.

Arizona Youth Contest - Grade 3 - First Place
Isabella Cote ~ Scottsdale, Arizona
Sonoran Sky Elementary School

Running Horse

A pretty dun horse
Galloping through clear water
Wind in her long mane

Arizona Youth Contest - Grade 4 - Second Place
Masyn Welker ~ Phoenix, Arizona
Sahuaro Elementary School

Born

I was born
I was born to do the impossible
I was born to create something new
I was born to change lives
I was born to make a change
I was born to help the world
I was born to make a difference
I was born to take to the skies
I was born to let my imagination grow
I was born to live with freedom
I was born to take one step at a time
I was born to make things
I was born to go past the limits
I was born to make magic
I was born

Arizona Youth Contest - Grade 3 - Third Place
Raffaella Benaglio ~ Scottsdale, Arizona
Black Mountain Elementary School

Loneliness

Loneliness is gray.
It sounds like nothing is there.
It smells like emptiness.
It tastes like bitter tears.
It looks like a broken heart.
Loneliness feels like you could disappear and nobody would
    notice.

ARIZONA YOUTH CONTEST
Grades 5-8

Judged By

Janine P. Dubik

Janine P. Dubik has been selected for Poetry in Transit, a program of the Luzerne County Transportation Authority, since 2016. Her poems have been published by *Pennsylvania Bards Eastern PA Poetry Review 2023, Poets Live Fourth Anthology, Manuscript 2021-2022 (and 2022-2023), Poets Live Third Anthology, The Scop, Back Channels'* "The Pandemic Issue," *Word Fountain, The Electric Rail,* and *Thirty-Third Wheel.* Janine's short stories have appeared in *Door = Jar* literary magazine and *Otherwise Engaged Literature and Art Journal.* A freelance copy editor/proofreader for Etruscan Press, she has an MFA in creative writing from Wilkes University, Wilkes-Barre, Pennsylvania. She resides with her husband, Mark, and their three cats in Northeastern Pennsylvania.

Arizona Youth Contest - Grade 6 - First Place
Meenasiam Clark ~ Kingman, Arizona
Kingman Academy of Learning Middle School

Dear Starchild

I have observed your growth.
One of few, you are special.
Moondust continues to fill your lungs,
And the stars continue to glitter back in your eyes.
You are the pride of the cosmos.

Shed your tears,
Drinking the poison
Your very own mind had poured.
Forgetting that, like the moon,
We must go through many phases of emptiness
In order to feel full again.

My darling starchild,
For a star to be born into existence,
Only one thing must occur,
A nebula must cave in.

So collapse.
Crumble.
This is not your end.

This is your birth.

Arizona Youth Contest – Grade 7 - Second Place
Grace Diane Blankenship ~ Avondale, Arizona
Fine Arts Academy

As The Rain Trickles Down The Drain

Rain trickles down the drain
A car races by
Change is hard
That's what they say
It's not supposed to be this way

I was supposed to be at the top,
at the top of the mountain
But as the rain pours
It becomes more clear
That I'm the rain, slowly being washed away

From mountains to the valleys
Change is hard
I can't accept it
Is it my fault?
Am I the problem?

I don't know why it changed
I left it undisturbed, unbroken
Just like a rain drop it shattered with disturbance

But why?
I wait for a reply
Those dreaded dots appear
They pause
And then they're gone.

I changed.
They're the same.
I am not.

Arizona Youth Contest – Grade 5 - Third Place
Levi Olbert ~ Yuma, Arizona
Dorothy Hall Elementary

Waterparks

Wet wild waterparks woosh my worries away
The thrill of entering the park entices me to play

I love the feel of crashing
I love the sound of splashing

This is the time of summer and the music of fall
I love the 5-foot diving board GA-DOOSH CANNONBALL

Slipping down the slide, my hands sway in the air
When I hit the bottom, water explodes in my hair

Spinning in a circus bowl
Plunging down the deep dark hole

At the end of the day, a lazy river makes its way
Relaxed and floating, the last feelings in the bay

Walking to my car, the sun sets in the west
This perfect day, was undoubtedly the best

ARIZONA YOUTH CONTEST
Grades 9 - 12

Judged By

Holly Parsons

Holly Parsons, mystic and spiritual seeker, studied journalism at San Diego State University, worked in journalism for a number of years and is the former publisher and managing editor of Idyllwild Life Magazine. Holly reads her poetry throughout the southwestern US, NYC and Dublin, Ireland. She is published in several anthologies including the *Arizona Centennial Poetry Anthology 2012* and *Blue Guitar*. Holly has been honored by the President of Ireland [Michael Higgins] for her poem honoring the life of acting educator Deirdre O'Connell, and for 5 years acted as a judge for The Phoenix Sister Cities International Poetry contest for disabled adults. She was poet laureate for the Cultural Arts Coalition, and is now a member of Idyllwild's Evolutionary Poets and an active participant in 10,000 Waves of Women Writers. Her poetry graces the pages of numerous corporate and community websites.
http://HollyParsons-poet.com/

Arizona Youth Contest - Grade 11 - First Place
Jacqueline Reyes ~ Phoenix, Arizona
Metro Tech High School

Achilles' Glory

For his glory,
I ran.
For what a terrible death
It would be without the chase.
Behind me, the incomparable Achilles
For ahead of me, my birthplace
Of Troy.

For his glory,
I stopped.
For what coward would run away?
Empowered–I stood!
As he approached,
His bloody footprints
Poached the battlefield.
My comrades would be carried under his feet
His heel hidden from sight.
I launched my spear
Into the empty abyss beside him.

For his glory,
I missed.
Awaiting Hades–now
I reminisce.
It was not a lack of skill,
For it was Zeus' will.
My aim was perfect!
My talent was unmatched!
My strength was unwavering!
But–
For his glory,
My spear did not pierce him.

Arizona Youth Contest - Grade 12 - Second Place
Julia Keefer ~ Tucson, Arizona
University High School

a hawk prepares to eat

jackrabbit,
you look so red against that bush
there are so many sorts of red
in this world:
crimson & cinnabar & terracotta
& you are all of them

how does it feel to be here
& there & all around,
all at once?
how does it feel to make up in leg
what you lack in brush?

you've lived a life of consequence - so much worry placed on stride

how does it feel to know
that you'll make up in wind
what you lack in hue?

the reflections in your eyes
will not return to bite you

of this time left
you must try to stay calm

the desert will learn to be red in your absence

run -

this desert will not blow away

Arizona Youth Contest - Grade 10 - Third Place
Suhani Varshney ~ Phoenix, Arizona
Pinnacle High School

A Day in the Life of an Afghan Girl

They returned so suddenly on a bright, sunny day
Like unexpected rain.
They snatched my freedom along with every other woman's.
It felt as if my wings had been clipped.
They made sure I was confined in my home.
The door became a barrier that blocked me from conquering
    the world.
For if I dared to stride outside they wouldn't hesitate to strike me
With brute force and rifle butts.

I had never felt fear like that, and I never intended to again
So now I will rebel.
For every girl deserves her rights.
For every girl fighting this torture with me is a hero.
I will protest this ignominy
Of which I am not deserving.

I refuse to wake up to the sound of more locks clicking shut
But to open my eyes and see my friend's faces without a burqa on.
To be able to choose the clothes I want to wear,
And steer my life in the direction I want.
For then I will be able to show the world who I truly am.

I will not take orders from him anymore.
I will determine my own future,
And help make sure that every other girl has a chance to see
The day where that sun will shine bright for them.

William Moody
Crane Landing

2023 ANNUAL CONTEST

This contest is open to members and non-members!

Qualifications are original, unpublished poems (except Category 13) not currently submitted to other contest(s). Any number of poems may be entered in each category, but individual poems may be submitted only once per entire contest. All entries should be sent in at one time. Submissions without fees will be disqualified.

Categories

1. ASPS Award
2. Aging Award
3. Ekphrastic Award
4. Our Changing Environment Award
5. Five C's of Arizona Award
6. Gardening Award
7. Haiku Award
8. Humor Award
9. Jessie Belle Rittenhouse Memorial Award
10. Legacy Award
11. Native Lands and/or Voices Award
12. Nature's Metaphor Award
13. Previously Published Poem Award
14. Previously Rejected Poem Award
15. Prose Poem Award
16. Rhyming Poetry for Children Award
17. Sci-Fi / Fantasy Award
18. Shakespearean Award
19. TAPS Award
20. Traditional Rhyme Award
21. Western Theme Award
22. Wild Places, Open Spaces Award

Prize Awards

Category 1	Categories 2-22
First Place ~ $100	First Place ~ $50
Second Place ~ $65	Second Place ~ $30
Third Place ~ $35	Third Place ~ $20

ANNUAL CONTEST

Category 1 ~ ASPS Award

Sponsored by the Arizona State Poetry Society

Judged by Jessica Rich

Jessica Rich lives in Missoula, MT. She is a writer and performer whose work has been included in *The Gravity of the Thing*, *River & South Review*, *Slaying The 10-Minute Play*, and other publications. Her chapbook of micropoems, *"Entomology & Salt"* can be found at Rinky Dink Press. She has performed her work across the country and was part of the Ping Chong project, "Unconditional," at Profile Theatre in Portland, Oregon. She also served on the selection committee for Weird Sisters' micro-grant, which awards artists on the Oregon Coast money for their projects, and on the 2018 AWP panel on performance. Jessica is currently working on her memoir, a novel, and two poetry manuscripts.

Category 1: ASPS Award
First Place: Stephen Bochinski ~ Oceanside, California

The Whale That Swallowed Me

Here I am
belched up
on the beach
of my existence
feeling around
in grains of sand
for bits and pieces
that I lost
washed out on
the outgoing tide.
I lie empty
as the stomach
of the whale
that swallowed me
a wordless message
on my lips
halting syllables
of my yearning
for the ocean
heaving in the night
my dream memory
now just saltwater
on my skin
slowly drying
but I can still hear
that whale singing.

Last Swim

It might have been a Tuesday,
but that's not important. Not really.
All she knew
was that when she looked at her pool
it looked more like a blue-tiled picture frame
than a destination.

She had no desire to get in.
No pull to feel her arms slice through the flat coolness;
no anticipation of floating on her back
watching flickers work their way up the palms;
no wondering about where the tiny planes might be going
or who they might be taking there.

There was only a noticing.

A brief thought that maybe the last time
was the last time.
That she should have marked it on her calendar
like all those social events,
due dates,
doctors' appointments,
first days of school,
fall days her barn swallows left for Mexico,
spring days they came back, and

long lost friends' birthdays.

Maybe she'd do it later.
The calendar was on the fridge in the kitchen
and final Jeopardy was about to begin.

Yukon Summer

One wild sweet summer I grew
on a ripe thorn of raspberry,
flowered in sun.

In my prodigal hour
I rose on a cloud of mayflies
through vermilion air
loudly humming,
reeling, unreeling gold tendrils
of midnight sun.

In my hour of sun
I tongued purple honey of asters,
drank fireweed wine
and danced
a frenzy of night on goldenrod
stamens of long light.

Dancing to morning,
tiring
of light, a small seed,
I am suddenly still
in white of caribou moss,
sinking down ...

down softer than a boreal owl
or willow ptarmigan,
deeper than a raven's night,
more silent than star petals
falling
to flower on snow.

Kim Sosin
Arizona Female Cardinal

ANNUAL CONTEST

Category 2 ~ Aging Award

Sponsored by Walter and Regina Ralston

Judged by Jiwon Choi

Jiwon Choi is the author of *One Daughter is Worth Ten Sons* and *I Used To Be Korean*. both published by Hanging Loose Press. She is an early childhood educator at the Educational Alliance where she works with children and teachers on developing emergent curriculum. She is a long-time gardener and coordinator at the Pacific Street Brooklyn Bear's Garden where she started her garden's first poetry reading series, *Poets Read in the Garden*, to support local poets with live reading events in a safe, outdoor space. You can find out more about her at iusedtobekorean.com.

Amaryllis Magnifica

In the midst of a dark,
cold Wisconsin winter,
Dad retrieves the amaryllis

from the basement.
He adds water,
and by some miracle,

the bulb in its pot
begins to sprout on the counter inside—
when it's below zero outside.

By early February
two thick green stalks rise, one
with buds protruding like mule's ears.

Daily we watch
the amaryllis evolve,
noting any slight changes.

Near the end of the month,
seven salmon-colored blooms—
as big as my hand—gloriously open.

The trumpet-shaped flowers
herald their triumphal entry
into the room,

a welcome distraction
from the slow recovery and healing
of Mom's brain surgery.

Then the other three-foot stem
prepares to produce, hopefully
on February 28, Mom's 85th birthday.

Low Arc

The pole beans
and sweet potato vines
lie diminished
after last night's frost.
A dying ladybug
lands on my leg.
I too am a day older,
here under the low arc
of November's sun.

Calculations

> *How many days are left of my life?*
> Kim Addonizio, "The Numbers"

I refuse to ask myself
about the lifespan of relatives,
family members long passed.
Instead, I plan ahead—
next summer's cruise on the Rhône
an outing soon to Mt. Lemmon
tomorrow's tostados at Mosaic.

To-do lists rattle in my head—
check round-trip fares to Paris
buy tickets for the symphony
order a book of poetry,
Mary Oliver perhaps.

Keep going I tell myself.
Don't count the days.

Kim Sosin
Snow Egret Breeding Plumage

ANNUAL CONTEST

Category 3 ~ Ekphrastic Award

Sponsored by NavWorks Press

Judged by Frances Cheong

Frances Cheong was born and raised in Hong Kong. She has studied and lived in Singapore, England, and various cities in the United States. She received her PhD in molecular cell biology at Johns Hopkins University and taught and directed undergraduate genetics courses at University of Washington for ten years. With a long-standing interest in literature and writing, Frances has been a Hugo House student in fiction and nonfiction writing since 2013, and is currently the Program Director for Education. She lives in Seattle and is working on a story collection.

Adam & Eve: After the Fall

*In response to "The Rebuke of Adam and Eve" by
Domenichino, 1626*

When God commenced Creation,
He thought, "It's not complicated,"
and He was *mostly* right.
He said, "Let there be light,"
and there was light—
then He made everything.

But what was He thinking
when He made that fruit
and then forbade it?
Was it that hard to predict
original sin would follow
such temptation, then end
like a Stanford experiment?

As God delivers his rebuke,
lions lick at unsuspecting sacrificial lambs—
first man shrugs
to blame first woman,
first woman points
to a limbless instigator
slithering back to its tree.

By the time God departs
in His cherubic carriage,
the serpent reaches a branch
to watch the aftermath unfold.
Imagine
their stunted conversation,
the carnage—
 reddened wool along a lion's jaw,
  bloodied bruises on Eve's,
 a broken rib, a serpent's sibilant signal
  as it slithers down to strike her.

Flamingo Gate

I have never been admitted to this garden
but I find my way often to the Flamingo Gate
and stand wondering
if beyond those vividly pink doors
lie fields of flowers more lush
than the ones that frame the approach

Carpets of gold and purple blossom
curve in graceful profusion
Hollyhocks flank the gate
and Italian cypress stand sentinel within the wall
Shadows of the trees behind me
dapple the white stucco with lavender

Charmed by this radiance
tantalized by its color and light
I wait here, wondering
if the serenity it seems to promise
can be mine,
this side of the flamingo gate.

In response to "Flamingo Gate," Theodore Van Soelen
https://www.bing.com/search?q=Bing+Images+Flamingo+Gate+painting

Gustave Caillebotte's *THE FLOOR SCRAPERS*

The splinters
are the least of it.
our backs have ached
since we were boys
blessed to be strong enough
to survive
the scourge of disease,
the rotting claw of hunger-
strong enough to work
until callused fingers bled
through dusty bandages
because there are no handouts
only labor, life, longing.

We work with our hands
but it is a fragile arrangement
we are an injury away
from starvation
from being street trash
kicked aside by a politician's boot.
pale skin and bone tired
strong sinewy, shapes
bend like broken cranes.
we cut, curl, scrape
as pieces of soul
fragments of flesh
fancy the floors
of a splendid room.

This will be a beautiful room.
one day, I will pass on the street
look up and be proud.
for now, the pungent smell
of varnish burns the nostrils
and we are sepia shadows
shaping the dreams of tomorrow.

Jon Sebba
Pollination

ANNUAL CONTEST

Category 4 ~ Our Changing Environment Award

Sponsored by Scottsdale Mustang Poets

Judged by Scott Lowery

Scott Lowery's poems appear in numerous print and online journals, including *Prairie Schooner, River Styx, Nimrod, Pinyon, RockPaperPoem,* and *Ocotillo Review.* He has been awarded the Julia Darling Memorial Poetry Prize, Pushcart and Best of Net nominations, and a residency at the Anderson Center. *Empty-handed* won the Emergence Chapbook Prize from Red Dragonfly Press (2013). Lowery's second chapbook, *Mutual Life* (Finishing Line, 2023), documents everyday life during tumultuous times. A 30-year veteran public school teacher, Lowery has presented writing workshops to young poets from grade school through college. Two of his teaching poems appear in *Stronger Than Fear* (Cave Moon, 2022), an anthology of social justice poems. After nearly thirty years living among the river bluffs and valleys of southeastern Minnesota, Lowery and his wife Connie Blackburn recently moved to Milwaukee, drawn by the inexorable pull of young grandchildren. www.scottlowery.org

Cool Pool, Night, Dark Blue

Above, the moon becomes
    the winter eye
        of a clouded dragon.

North of desert mountains
    lightning barks
        into dark winds.

A hint of ozone singes
    and petrichor torments
        with a promise of rain.

Last night the moon
    was round in an undisturbed,
        cloud-ruckled, square sky;

the calm before the non-storm,
    uncertain of its welcome
        in the thirsty valley.

What Happened Today

I walk to the willows where geese dance,
a long-tailed skimmer bombs by. A piper bobtails
into marsh. The weather map shows 110°
but here it's cool and clean, no more
wildfire smoke. What will happen to us?

Purple coneflower, ox-eyed daisies, and bird's eye
trefoil punctuate the path, lead to a subset
of willows, black-eyed birch, cottonwood
shimmy. Should I sing?

The days are longer.
The northern lights come out tonight

Sailing in a Sinkhole

Is it the wind that has blown us here
or we adrift in uncertain waters,

caught in a nowhere tide? The moon
neither waxes or wanes, has no

gravitational pull or sway. We are
lost but not becalmed, these waters

are thick, they slow us down,
they are warming ice, volcanic sludge.

This is the worst poem I have ever
written, it drags at my feet

like invasive weed, tangles
my thoughts. I was trying to travel

away from here but my rudder
caught me up in the shallows.

When the poem says we,
it means I and when I say poem

I mean a frustrated dream,
I mean a ship full of holes slowly

sinking, I mean nothing.

Jon Sebba
Hummingbird

ANNUAL CONTEST

Category 5 ~ Five C's of Arizona Award
(Cattle, Citrus, Climate, Cotton, Copper)

Sponsored by West Valley Poets

Judged by Janna Knittel

Janna Knittel is the author of *Real Work* (Nodin, 2022), a finalist for the 2023 Minnesota Book Award in poetry and the chapbook *Fish & Wild Life* (Finishing Line, 2018). Janna has also published poems in *Blue Mountain Review, Constellations, North Dakota Quarterly, Pleiades, The Trumpeter*, and *The Wild Word* as well as the following anthologies: *Waters Deep: A Great Lakes Anthology* (Split Rock, 2018); *The Experiment Will Not Be Bound* (Unbound Edition, 2023); and *Broad Wings, Long Legs: A Rookery of Heron Poems* (North Star, 2023). Janna is also a current Minnesota State Arts Board grantee.

Don't Comfort Me With Apples

Mama and Daddy drove into town
leaving me one task only:
to keep the cows within the field.
"Don't let them get into the orchard.

Cows aren't smart enough to stop
when they are full. They would founder
on the apples and could die."
I nodded and marched to the pasture,

a five year old on a mission. And yet
the frogs were jumping, and the mint
along the ditch bank wanted me
to pick it and the clouds were so fine.

When I heard the car chug up the lane,
my head jerked up. I looked for the herd.
Oh, no! The cows were in the orchard,
gobbling apples. Daddy came running.

Mama brought the knife. Daddy pushed it
into each bloated stomach. Oh, the stench
as the contents spewed. Saved all but one,
never again would she sashay to the barn.

We piled up tumbleweeds and sagebrush,
poured gasoline all over her. My penance:
to feed the fire for tearful hours
until it was just a lump of embers

among the trees. At apple-picking time,
I tried to look anywhere except
that patch of cinders and wondered
whether a cow can forgive.

Category 5: Five C's of Arizona Award
Second Place: Linda Rittenhouse ~ Scottsdale, Arizona

Sonoran Circle

In climate of sun on sun on sun
cattle camp 'neath citrus trees.

Copperhead coil in chaparral,
await hot blood of cottontail.

Copper Mines

Cattle graze where houses
of miners once stood, some
shacks still there; weathered
boards falling in on themselves.

Copper mines dug into hillsides;
folks build cabins, patched holes
in walls with tin can lids; they
survived, hauling water two miles.

Climate was hot, except winter
when snow came through chinks
in the walls. Kids hiked to the
one-room school through drifts.

Food was sparse. No fresh fruit
or vegetables. Around Christmas,
father rode to town; parents filled
bags with candy, sometimes an
orange; bags were handed out
at church on Christmas Eve.

That night, children pulled scratchy
wool blankets up to the necks (never
soft cotton), dreamed of Santa coming
to their pitiful camp in the hills.

Gail Denham
Twisted Tree

ANNUAL CONTEST

Category 6 ~ Gardening Award

Sponsored by Laura Rodley

Judged by Christine Gelineau

Christine Gelineau is the author of three full-length books of poetry, most recently CRAVE (NYQ Books, 2016). Other books include the book-length sequence APPETITE FOR THE DIVINE, published as the Editor's Choice for the Robert McGovern Prize from Ashland Poetry Press, 2010 and REMORSELESS LOYALTY, winner of the Richard Snyder Memorial Prize, also from Ashland Poetry Press, 2006. A recipient of the Pushcart Prize, Gelineau's poetry, essays and reviews have appeared in numerous journals and anthologies, including *Prairie Schooner, New York Times, Connecticut Review, New Letters, Green Mountains Review, Georgia Review* and others. Gelineau teaches at Binghamton University, where she is Associate Director of the Creative Writing Program and coordinator of the Readers' Series. She also teaches in the low-residency graduate writing program at Wilkes University.

Category 6: Gardening Award
First Place: Jane Randall ~ Centerville, Utah

Zucchini Bread
(cinquain chain)

Straggly
August garden
full of weeds, zucchinis
(thick-skinned-twenty-pound zucchinis) --
past ripe.

Still, I'm
my mother's child
and mustn't let them waste
and thus confirm my failings, so
I reap

and scour
the dark green bombs
in search of worthy pith
that's fit to shred, although I doubt
it's there.

Except
it is! Enough
for several tender loaves
of moist and fragrant bread. I'm glad
for this

small boost
to my green thumb's
wilted morale. Reflect-
ing on *my* straggly, past-ripe pith,
I smile.

An Annual Admonition

"Yesterday is gone. Tomorrow has not yet come.
We have only today. Let us begin." — Mother Teresa

In early spring,
only memory hints of
revolving revival.
Instead of snow,
drizzling rain chills
the bones.
Seed catalogs and
gardening magazines
fill the mail box with
potential explosions of color,
renewal, warmth, life.
Perennials, planted once,
promise delphinium blue,
coreopsis gold and lobelia red
year after year, while
geraniums, impatiens, marigolds
and zinnias celebrate
only the present, as if to say
"Be wary of anyone who claims
that the way things are
is the way things will always be."

Raining on Weeds

What's so special about the rain?
Poets write it brings May flowers.
Do they ever write of the pain
sitting in my room for hours,
watching it splash on my window?
In April, Will would buy his seeds,
ten long years I've been his widow,
ten years it's been raining on weeds.

Kim Sosin
Arizona Finch

ANNUAL CONTEST

Category 7 ~ Haiku Award

Sponsored by Kenneth Pearson

Judged by Johnette Downing

Recipient of the Louisiana Writer Award, **Johnette Downing** is a haiku poet, and the co-founder of the former New Orleans Haiku Society. Her haiku have been widely published in journals such as *bottle rockets, Frogpond, Modern Haiku, Mayfly, Prune Juice, Red Moon Anthologies, World Haiku, tiny words, and O Muse!* to name a few. Her poem "ripples in the pond" received a Haiku International Association Honorable Mention Award in Japan. Her spring 2022 release, *Singing Waters, A Selection of Haiku, Senryu, and Haibun* from buddha baby press, is a collection of over one hundred of her previously published poems in one volume. johnettedowning.com

Category 7: Haiku Award
First Place: Martha H. Balph ~ Millville, Utah

twenty years gone --
still she brings to the grave
Christmas toys

poking between ribs
of the old buck's agony
wild irises

Category 7: Haiku Award
Third Place: Janice L. Freytag ~ Souderton, Pennsylvania

breathless August night
lightning cracks the sky open
letting in the wind

Kim Sosin
Male Red Winged Black Bird doing his Mating Call

ANNUAL CONTEST

Category 8 ~ Humor Award

Sponsored by East Valley Poets

Judged by Carolyne Wright

Carolyne Wright's most recent books are *Masquerade*, a memoir in po-
etry (Lost Horse Press, 2021), and *This Dream the World: New &
Selected Poems* (Lost Horse, 2017), whose title poem received a Pushcart
Prize and appeared in *The Best American Poetry*. She has nine earlier
books and chapbooks of poetry; a ground-breaking anthology, *Raising
Lilly Ledbetter: Women Poets Occupy the Workspace* (Lost Horse, 2015),
which received ten Pushcart Prize nominations; and five award-winning
volumes of poetry in translation from Spanish and Bengali. A
Contributing Editor for the Pushcart Prizes, Carolyne lived in Chile and
traveled in Brazil on a Fulbright Grant; on her return, she studied with
Elizabeth Bishop at the University of Washington. Carolyne returned to
Brazil in 2018 for an Instituto Sacatar artist's residency in Bahia. A
Seattle native who teaches for Richard Hugo House, she has received
grants from the NEA, 4Culture, and the Radcliffe Institute, among others.
A Fulbright U.S. Scholar Award to Brazil took her back to Salvador,
Bahia, in mid-2022; with another two months in 2024.

The Optometrist's Nemesis

Eye doctor says: "To get a start,
Look at the wall and read the chart."
I squint and try to do my part
In "seeing" what I know by heart:

"On top there's one enormous *E*!
It's followed by (I think) *F-P*.
The third row down says *T-O-Z* --
And under that, *L-P-E-D*."

The doctor's face begins to fall.
He clears his throat -- a deadly pall.
"I fear you have not passed at all.
The chart is on a different wall!"

A Toot's a Toot

We call then euphemistic names
like panty burp, butt flute,
but the whole world knows when stale wind blows
'cause a toot's a toot is a toot.

Ben Franklin told us, "Fart proudly!"
His T-shirt read, "Pop Pride."
Dozen a day the experts say,
don't keep heinie hiccups inside!

Why are we so embarrassed, Dear,
to give a bean salute,
or booty bomb at the senior prom?
'Cause a toot's a toot is a toot.

When under thunder brings brown clouds
There's honkers in the sky.
Your butt bazooka's done it's job
when back drafts float on by.

Those turtle burps beside the stream
and fanny frogs pollute.
Sorry, Sweet Earth, it can't be helped,
'cause a toot's a toot is a toot.

Air biscuits perk up happy hour.
Let loose and cut the cheese!
Just tell your loved ones, "pardon me"
in the wake of a good butt sneeze.

On, Rattler! On Ripper! On, Gasser! On, Whiff!
On, Squeaker! On, Puffer! On, Poot!
To the top of the roof, to the top of the wall!
'Cause a toot's a toot is a toot!

A Quiet Musing Coffee Morning

Formless. Reading the poetry of folks who won
When I didn't. What's better, what's worse?
At least I've found a safe spot in the sun
A place where I can make my lips rehearse

What I didn't win. What's better, what's worse?
Self-doubt is like the tide: comes in goes out
To where I make my lips rehearse
On something like a smile and less a pout.

Self-doubt is like the tide, comes in goes out,
All rhythms flicker within one heart beat
From something like a smile to more a pout,
Something not too sour, a psychic treat.

All rhythms cycle like the heart's strong beat.
Pound out from head to toe: It's me, me, me;
Something not too sour, a psychotic treat.
If no one ever sees it—well, it's meant to be.

Though nothing head to toe is me, me, me
Unvarying. I'm blended, split, perverse.
If no one ever sees that—well, it's meant to be
Just how I make my lips rehearse.

It's quite embarrassing to even mention this.
At least I've found a safe spot in the sun
For sharing my existential crisis:
Me—formless—reading the poetry of folks who won.

Gail Denham
Doorknob

ANNUAL CONTEST

Category 9 ~
Jessie Belle Rittenhouse Memorial Award

Sponsored by Linda Rittenhouse

Judged by Julia Johnson

Julia Johnson earned a BA from Hollins College and an MFA in creative writing from the University of Virginia, where she was a Henry Hoyns Fellow and studied under Rita Dove, Gregory Orr, and Charles Wright. She is the author of the poetry collections *Subsidence* (Groundhog Poetry Press, 2016), *The Falling Horse* (Factory Hollow Press, 2012), and *Naming the Afternoon*, (LSU Press, 2002), which won the Fellowship of Southern Writers George Garrett New Writing Award. Her poems have appeared or are forthcoming in *Tin House, Cincinnati Review, Poetry International, The Southern Poetry Anthology, Sentence: A Journal of Prose Poetics, Washington Square*, and numerous other journals and anthologies. Currently, she is Professor of English at the University of Kentucky, where she founded and directs the MFA in the Creative Writing Program. Prior to joining the faculty at Kentucky, she taught at Hollins University, University of North Carolina at Greensboro, and in the Center for Writers at the University of Southern Mississippi.

Rhymes with River

In spring, the willow extolls
the beauty of yellow,
with limbs that flex and roll
in the warming wind,
and the river follows,
relaxing its icy stance, it slows
and wallows,
twirls in foam-lipped eddies
and dances in the embrace
of mud-stuck stumps,
a foreshadowing
of the marriage of summer
rains with river's flow.
By autumn the yellow-tinged
branches of the willow
are stripped away by wind,
the remaining slender
leaves shiver at the river's edge,
slip from shore and skitter
into the water, glimmer there
like flecks of gold,
like so many wedding rings
tossed in the river, they
tumble and roll
in Autumn's last glow,
while winter rattles its icy chains
and wind billows cold
and sere, a bell that tolls
the close of the year.

First Love

Full August orb was rising
when he slipped out his back door
to wander past her window,
take a glance and nothing more.

For he knew her kindred spirit
wanted nothing of that room
on a night when tides pulled doubt aside
truth empowered by the moon

whose fullness and whose glory,
whose all-seeing golden face
replaced the throb of reason,
let emotion take its place.

Like an orchestrated ballet---
perfect timing crossing paths,
they met beside the river,
knew first love would be their last.

Hearts aligned like constellations,
counted days to reach eighteen.
Sweet futures flashed before them
through their open door of dreams.

Portal

> after "Harlem" by Langston Hughes

When did we have that dream?

> When the Crayola under our pillow was labeled
> *Peach__*   or *flesh*?
> when the book on the bedside table
> was outlined_ neuroscience
> absolute, or muddy_ parable
> of knights burning the savior's creche

Was this the dream we shared?

> Promised blessings about to bloom
> singing muffled in a vessel close to shore,
>
> musty generations in a crowded room
> *about to open the door*

Does the dream still matter?

> Swinging under the willow tree
> bare toes reaching for the moon,
> or obsolete
> thoughts tucked tight in wrinkled
> sheets
> bleached white by washboard scrubbing
> of sticky memory

Kim Sosin
Bluejay

ANNUAL CONTEST

Category 10 ~ Legacy Award

Sponsored by CChristy White

Judged by Stephen Bochinski

Stephen Bochinski began writing poetry after attending a creative writing class at Palomar College almost thirty years ago. His work can be found in *North of Oxford, The Pandemic Issue # 6, Medium,* where he posts regularly and in his self-published chap book *Psyche Trouble.* The natural world inspires him as well as the internal nature that is found in everyone. He counts himself fortunate to live in Oceanside, California where he can walk to the beach and get his feet wet in the waves that have traveled thousands of miles to arrive one after the other.

Hearts
Dedicated to Melanie

I cradle the ripeness of my body
picture your chalky curves on a black screen
dark hollows for eyes, a fluttering heart
beats, more wonderful than hummingbird wings.

When my body begins to still, yours wakes
we press our hands together like lovers
bidding farewell through a train window
I whisper "I love you" against the glass.

At first no larger than a grain of sand
or the period that ends this sentence.
Now the size of a grapefruit, an eggplant,
a melon, the empty space in my arms.

You arrive at last carrying my heart
with you out into the endless open.

In China

The terra cotta warriors
stand at eternal attention,
row upon row,
and, despite the emperor's intentions,
about as useful to him in the afterlife
as a phalanx of flowerpots.

I wonder, will the treasures
I intend to take with me -
moonlight on sculpted snowbanks,
scent of lilacs, swell of ancient hymns,
moments of grace and decades of love -
will they prove as futile,
as ultimately absurd,
as those pottery soldiers?
I don't know.
But like the emperor,
I continue to build my collection.

In His Last Days of Summer
To my husband

As you lie
in the interminable droning
of locusts, holding
to the last, dying and knowing --

do you even now
love beyond all reason
gold August grass?
do you weep for the locust
whose late summer pain sears the air
with singing?

You have loved me, always.
I do not ask more.

I have said good-bye
to the sun a thousand times
as if it were I, as if I
could be you --

am I what I mourn?

Michele Worthington
White Winged Doves Nest in Cactus

ANNUAL CONTEST

Category 11 ~ Native Lands and Voices Award

Sponsored by Lollie Butler

Judged by Jennifer Reeser

Jennifer Reeser has published seven books. X.J. Kennedy wrote that her debut "ought to have been a candidate for a Pulitzer." Her fourth was an Amazon Top Ten Best Seller. Her sixth, "INDIGENOUS," received "Best Poetry Book of 2019" from Englewood Review. *Publishers Weekly* calls *Strong Feather*, "an excellent collection...full of artistry and meaning." She is a three-time winner of *RATTLE*'s "Poets Respond." Her work has appeared in *POETRY, The Hudson Review, RATTLE, The Lyric,* and elsewhere. Her anthologies include Random House London's "Everyman's Library" series. She has received seven nominations for the Pushcart. Her Russian translations are authorized by FTM Agency, Moscow. Her poetry has been translated into many languages and has been featured at the POETRY Foundation. A.M. Juster calls her "...our top Native American poet." She is a bi-racial writer of European/Native American Indian ancestry. She studied at McNeese and has served at the West Chester Conference. https://jenniferreeser.com/

Badlands at Sundown

It is Monday in mid-July.
Sunset arrives in The Badlands.
I sit on a rocky grey spire
And let the wind wash me clean,
Like some mystical rite of reset,
Fancying this breeze as the breath of God.

I've invited my fiends to this place,
But they don't seem to want to fight me here,
And I'm not at all disappointed,
Choosing instead to bask in the peace
That ensues as my demons default.

I think maybe it was a place like this,
With its unique, desolate beauty,
Where Jesus dealt with his Devil
And walked away victorious.
Or the voice of some Sioux Shaman
Singing hymns to the power of this place
Much like a stream in the Smokies
When I knew who protected me there.
And I wish that I could stay,
But the sun runs away to the west,
And, sadly unable to follow,
To pursue its life and light,
Then, as it steals to its next locale
It leaves me that one star, my star,
And it seems alone, and musing, like me,
And for a time it is only us
And we greet each other like brothers
Until the big dipper arrives in force
And pours the sky full of stars.

And as Tuesday seems apparent,
I am left with just my muses,
And the gentle breath of God,
Glorying in another sanctuary
Where I will sleep in Elysium
With one thought on my mind-

Each day should die this happily.

Indian Joe

I do not know his tribe.
Was he Menominee,
was he Winnebago,
or was he Stockbridge-Munsee
come up the river from Shawano?
Indian Joe. That was the name they gave him
when they sold him a sand farm in Oconto County.
The farm was his, but it fought him. Sixty acres of weeds and
scrub pine boxed by gravel roads no one plowed.
Soil too poor for corn. He hauled black muck from the pond
in a red wheel barrow dripping green water,
hauled it to the kitchen garden on the hill,
fed the muck to the sand to make it fertile,
tossed algae to the boney chickens who spilled from the lean-to,
nothing but clucks and beaks and feathers.
And when he was gone, I do not know who it was that came in the night
to wrap his body in burlap, to lay him out gently as you lay a baby to sleep,
to raise him high on a birch wood scaffold.
Who was it who banged the drum, who pounded the birch poles
into red earth at the edge of the hopeless field.
Who was it who made sure that all would see him
cradled, loved, raised up to join the spirit race,
to temp crows but deny coyotes, skinny chickens dangling limp and
companionable from the pallet, lifting Indian Joe higher in death
than he was allowed in life.

Ojibwa Spirit

Three cedar flutes:
The one I treasure most
shows the long scissor-bill,
the noble red-and-white head
of a whooping crane.
If you are moved
to admire, even revere her
for the beauty of that head,
this flute will deceive you.

She sings in a tongue
not of Crane, but another ancient--
Great Northern Diver,
Loon.
Her unearthly cry
wafts across a dark lake
when Great Bear circles the polestar
and the scent of spruce hangs heavy
in frosted air.
If you draw up a blanket and sit awhile,
her sister, White-throated Sparrow,
will pipe a mournful reply.
Their voices will dance
back and forth through the night
to the spectral beat
of Aurora Borealis.

Three flutes:
Two are carved as loons;
the other, a crane.
Only one
is possessed by that voice
Ojibwa hold sacred--
Brave Spirit,
Loon Spirit,
Mahng.

John Sebba
Crane Feeding

ANNUAL CONTEST

Category 12 ~ Nature's Metaphor Award

Sponsored by Tucson Poetry Society

Judged by Sally Badawi

Sally Badawi is an Arab American poet whose words appear in *Hayden's Ferry Review, Diode, Cream City Review and* elsewhere. She is a Tin House Workshop graduate and a recipient of a poetry fellowship from Summer Literary Series. Her work has been nominated for Best of the Net, the Pushcart Prize, and the Nina Riggs Poetry Award. She lives in the pacific northwest where she teaches writing at Portland Community College.

Category 12: Nature's Metaphor
First Place: Michael Spears ~ Sandy, Utah

Wild Asparagus

Long before the horses ran
in fields wet with dew,
before buried concrete pipe
replaced the weedy irrigation ditch,
before daffodils and red-tinged tulips
blossomed along the eastern bank,
wild asparagus grew.
The best part of spring,
end of March to early May,
was harvesting of tawny spears
piercing through damp, decomposed soil.
Armed with bucket, gloves and serrated knife,
every third morning without fail,
my wife or I would slip the blade beneath
the turf, stemming succulent slender stalks.
Garlic fields now wane downwind where
the old Sicilian farmed wet ground.
Wild asparagus disappeared
when concrete pipe was laid.
Neighbors came with shovels, rakes
and wheelbarrows loaded with dirt
spared from unused gardens where
potatoes, melons and flowers flourished.
Springtime now brings red-tinged tulips
and daffodils facing windy field.
Like horses, there's something in the magic
of wild asparagus roaming free.

Category 12: Nature's Metaphor Award
Second Place: Gurupreet K. Khalsa ~ Mobile, Alabama

I'm Writing a Lecture on Validity and Reliability

And our ears are sound/ tuning into themselves/
--Lenard D. Moore, "A Bluesman's Blues"

It takes some silence, concentration;
Carl Sandburg said, *knowing silence*
will bring all one way or another
so I'm waiting for the all to come

but the mockingbird is singing;
he sings and sings and sings
and a train whistles across the trees;
winds rustle leaves in feathery counterpoint

to distant cars on the freeway;
could be ocean surf, surround sound
undergirding the scritch of my pencil
and breathing rasping through my nose,

and the mockingbird keeps singing;
my refrigerator hums, gurgles,
something tap-taps out of sight,
a scolding bird joins in chorus;

a siren, some emergency not mine,
now two, rowr-rowr-rowr-your-boat
rendition, now horns, shrill shrieks
not unlike the whistle inside my head;

what begins as low thrums crescendos
to cicada-like anthem percussing
the afternoon, riding a wave;
and the mockingbird sings

the reliability of renewal, as leaves
release in autumn and bud
again in Spring, regeneration
and the validity of bird-song.
                    (Carl Sandburg, "The Answer")

Nesting

The bird is back,
Building unwise nest
In empty cardboard box
On our front porch,
Not a place suited
To raising babies
Safely,
But each year,
She tries,
Nesting in some strange
Man-made orifice,
A herald of Spring
And choices
Made in an imperfect
World,
And each year,
There are no birdlings,
Nest eventually
Abandoned
Due to the commotion
Of our comings
And goings,
Inevitable from the start,
I guess,
But it must be Spring again,
Because she's trying.

Jon Sebba
Waddling Couple

ANNUAL CONTEST

Category 13 ~ Previously Published Poem Award

Sponsored by: Alan and Kris Perry

Judged by Sally Lehman

Sally K Lehman is the author of the novels *The Last Last Fight* (Black Bomb Books), *In The Fat* (Black Bomb Books), *The Unit – Room 154*, and *Living in the Second Tense*. Her serialized short story *Small Minutes* was included in the Best Of edition of *Bewildering Stories*, and her story *Barren* was released through Write Out Publishing. She is also the editor of the anthologies *Bear the Pall, War Stories 2016,* and *War Stories 2017*. Her work can be found in multiple literary magazines including *The Coachella Review, Another Chicago Magazine, Lunch Ticket, The Bangalore Review*, and *34th Parallel*. Sally has an M.F.A. in Creative Writing from Wilkes University where she worked as Managing Editor for *River & South Review*. She lives in Portland, Oregon.

Category 13: Previously Published Poem Award
First Place: Charity Everitt ~ Tucson, Arizona

Unpacking the Cartons, I Find Your Coffee Mug

From stiff white paper I unfold the coverlet
that was my wedding gift to you.
The work of my hands, I can't unravel it;
at night I sleep under it, almost without pain.

You say you will crate and ship my rocker –
you've finished others and don't need mine
to prove your skill. The hard Missouri walnut
held me long nights I could not hold you.

Unpacking the cartons, I find your coffee mug,
the one that says "Pilot," last reminder
of hours we welded and riveted to build
an airplane we were, in the end, afraid to fly.

You are the craftsman skilled with hands
and sharp tools; show me how to chisel
what is you from my bones, what solvent will strip
you from my blood. Tell me how to turn
your shaping from the cells of my brain

and I will not be anyone either of us knows.

Previously published in *Her Words*, Winter 2021

reunion of old lovers

after *Reunion* by Megan Fernandes

odd interface—potentiometers of patience
dashboard lights blink in disbelief the plane
has made it around the world again—here
we are at the starting point—but the sun
has moved into a garage with room
for only my Prius—we move to say something
then stop—realize the old philosopher
is right—the waters of this river are different now—
and so are we—and so are we

Previously published in *Jasper's Folly,* April 2023

Day Breaking

Within the corridor dividing night
From day, I dreamed I found a unicorn
And lay beneath the shadow of his horn.
Akin to sorrow was his shade -- not quite
Beginning to be gold, and neither white
Nor gray, but color waiting to be borne
Away as dawn awakes: I too shall mourn
That indigo receding into light

Now losing night, Aurora bares her fire.
Above, young steeds run wild, as Phaethon
Pursues a dream to which he must aspire:
Discovery, some say, begins at dawn.
But who's to heed the rage of sun's desire?
My love is of the night, and night is gone.

Previously published in *Touchstone*, 1994

Kim Sosin
Arizona Gila Woodpecker

ANNUAL CONTEST

Category 14 ~ Previously Rejected Poem Award

Sponsored by: William Moody

Judged by Mary Jo Robinson-Jamison

Mary Jo Robinson-Jamison lives in St. Paul, Minnesota where she and her husband, Kent, raised their two children. She worked with the severely multiply handicapped as a music therapist for forty years. Her poems have been published in *Eastern Iowa Review*, *Still Point Arts Quarterly*, *Driftwood Press*, *Talking Writing*, *Talking Stick*, *Minnesota Voices*, and others.

Voyager

I found you on a moon of Mars
following trails of frozen canals

distant from a sea of tranquility.
Propelled into solar storms

through a cloudy telescope, I calculated
orbits of when we'd meet, wondering

if this trip was too far to return.
Your red glow flared on the horizon

but a core attraction held me –
a thaw in your icy landscape.

I scanned for an earthrise
above your mountainous shoulders

as you paused, rotating until
all I saw was shadow.

Alone like an exoplanet,
I want to know if you will stay

on this rock in deep space,
breathe its thin atmosphere

with me, find the next sign of life.
Or will you leave the ash of us –

stone and dust of what's come before –
and search for another distant satellite

invisible to the naked eye
but always moving, circling?

Monsoons

Witness the sudden advance of clouds
marching gray specters
darken the sky.

Now rain falls
silver ropes
tethering earth to the heavens.

Swollen horizon
cracked open by lightning
honeysuckle releases her sweet breath.

All sound is thunder and water
the echo of a language
we thought we'd forgotten.

Double Helix Tattoo

Numb, walking through the supermarket
I put random things in my cart, ignoring my list
Shopping is a thing I need to do. I have a list.
Sleeping is another thing I need to do, but
I need to keep track of things on the outside too
My forays outside of the hospital are fast and few.
My forehead briefly touches the door of the case,
It seems silly to price frozen peaches, but I do.
Most rooms on Seven West have mothers
The hospital advertises itself as "family friendly"
Which makes it sound like a franchise diner
Serving comfort food for affordable prices.
Rooms on Seven West have fold up beds for family.
We are given refrigerator space and places to bathe.
We can do laundry. We can maintain. We manage.
Mornings in the coffee room, some of us, talk
About how "we" are responding to treatment
Or when "our" next surgery is scheduled.
Identities and interests of family members merge
With those of the patients, our imperiled children..
We tell each other how lucky we are but it's a lie.
The great research hospital is justly renowned
But lucky children never end up there.
The world's best hospitals are not about luck.

The supermarket express line is closed..
Not yet sufficiently enlightened to welcome
Another opportunity to resign myself
To circumstances beyond my control,
 I shut my eyes and take a breath before
Taking my place at the back of a long line.
The man ahead of me lifts his left arm.
His arm bears a tattoo, an elegant double helix
In black, a twisted ladder with 23 rungs.
The pattern has one flaw, not easy to spot.
His wrist bears the color-coded hospital band
Given to repeat visitors on the pediatric floor.
My own band is hidden by a ruffled sleeve.

Kim Sosin
Bird Feeder at Tohona Chul Park

ANNUAL CONTEST

Category 15 ~ Prose Poem Award

Sponsored by: Janet McMillan Rives

Judged by Mona Lisa Saloy

Mona Lisa Saloy, Ph.D., is the new Louisiana Poet Laureate, an award-winning author & folklorist, educator, and scholar, of Creole culture in articles, documentaries, and poems about Black New Orleans. Currently Conrad N. Hilton Endowed Professor and of English at Dillard University, her first book, *Red Beans & Ricely Yours*, won the T.S. Eliot Prize and the PEN/Oakland Josephine Miles Award. Her book, *Second Line Home* is a collection of poems that captures day-to-day New Orleans speech, family dynamics, celebrates New Orleans, and gives insight into the unique culture the world loves. She was featured recently at Poets House, New York City. Check out the new issue of the *Chicago Quarterly Review*, an *Anthology of Black American Literature*, Volume 33, 2021. Tweet: @RedBeanSista www.monalisasaloy.com

"The Mere Distinction of Color"
--James Madison

In the South Yard of Montpelier, dried grass and rotting railroad ties lie above the graves of the enslaved who served the Madisons. Over 100 in number, they labored day and night, putting up crops, smoking hams, plowing fields, Joe and Sawney most mentioned, and others whose kin was sold, whose bitter tears made no difference to the president who Hated slavery and loved liberty on paper only. Cracked, ashy hands detasseled corn, grafted vines, patted red soil around berry beds, strung beans, kept cold the ice, hot the soup, cool the chambers. They slept squashed together in quarters on floor and sacks, up with the sun to do it all over--again and again and again, Dolley in feathered turbans ordered Sarah, Sukey, and Ellen in rag scarves, who watched and waited for freedom's road, hands busy polishing silver, churning cream. South Yard excavators have recreated two cabins, a kitchen, and a smokehouse far away from the plantation house where Madison squinted over the Bill of Rights, gazed at blue mountains from sparkling windows. Beneath the yard, hundreds of moldering forms lie buried, unmoving as they never were in life, resting, unafraid of the lash at last, the Madisons' granite obelisk casting a long shadow over the unmarked.

Hombre Mucho Grande

Grandpa grew up in Mexico in the colonies among his thirty-two siblings (yes, thirty-two) and their three mothers. He spoke Spanish like a native and probably felt like one. He grew apples, cherries, and plums, hauled them to Arizona and then brought back citrus and melons in his rusty old International truck. We would hear him chugging up the lane and run barefoot through the dust hollering, "Yay! Grandpa's back." Then he would lower the tailgate and start handing out the broken melons. We gorged on their dripping hearts and spit seeds at each other, sitting on the crab grass lawn or swinging from the tire hung from a cottonwood limb.

He was usually pretty easy going, but when he got riled, you would hear a string of Spanish and know it was not polite talk. Grandma would turn red and hush him. If we got out of line, he would just say, "Silencio! You savvy? You savvy?" We'd duck our heads, trying to look small, and mumble, "Si, Grandpa, we savvy."

As a kid, I thought he was a big man. The last time I saw him I was puzzled to see this fragile old guy in a too-large shirt. I wondered what had changed him, couldn't see that I was the one who had changed. Oh, Grandpa.

Category 15: Prose Poem Award
Third Place: Terry Judy Miller ~ Richmond, Texas

How to Save the World

Let the leaves do the telling when we're all dead and gone. Every hundred years there are nine billion people who weren't here one-hundred years before. So how does that old hatred keep springing new if mankind changes flesh every hundred years? I tell you what the seeds from my satsuma orange tell me—*someone plants—something grows*. Choose wisely when you open the hearts of your children to sow what you've learned of the vicious, wicked world. Tell them they are the hope—the tree from which peace will bloom—love them into their re-sponsibility.

Kim Sosin
Female Red Winged Blackbird

ANNUAL CONTEST

Category 16 ~ Rhyming Poetry for Children Award

Sponsored by: Elaine A. Powers

Judged by Susan Hood

Susan Hood is the award-winning author of many children's books in verse including *Alias Anna, Double Take, Leaps and Bounce, Lifeboat 12, The Last Straw: Kids vs. Plastics, Harboring Hope, Rooting for You, Shaking Things Up,* and *We Are One.* She has been honored with an E.B. White Read Aloud Picture Book Honor, two Christopher Awards, the Américas Award for Children's and Young Adult Literature, the Golden Kite Award, the Bank Street Flora Stieglitz Straus Award, given annually for "a distinguished work of nonfiction," and an NCTE Notable Poetry Book Award. Visit her at www.susanhoodbooks.com.

Category 16: Rhyming Poetry for Children Award
First Place: Linda Rittenhouse ~ Scottsdale, Arizona

Meadow

Dear Hilly Meadow,
   sweet meadow so wild,
Do you remember
   when I was a child?

I raced through your grasses
   as high as my knees;
inhaled purple clover
   along with your bees.

Made crowns with your daisies
   and friends with your birds.
Learned the language of crickets
   and practiced their words.

You held me and whispered
   while I gazed at the clouds.
You kept all my secrets
   when the world got too loud.

You caught buckets of tears
   when they spilled off my face.
Kissed my cheeks 'til I giggled
   with Queen Anne's white lace.

I thank you, Dear Meadow,
   sweet meadow so wild,
for loving me no
   matter what as a child.

An Honest Appraisal of Ballet Class

Buns are for burgers, not for your hair.
Pink leotards are torture to wear.
The moves are French, the tunes are Russian,
They lack any trace of bass or percussion.
The teacher's Napoleon, reincarnated;
I wish that her lessons were better translated.
We *pliéd* and *chasséd* til quarter to noon
When I gratefully leapt my way out of the room.

Kitchen Concert

When all the house is fast asleep,
I hear them all night long,
The ketchup, mustard, pickles
And the milk burst into song,

From deep inside our mighty "fridge,
They've carried on for years,
Of course when onions start to sing,
I cover up my ears!

Who'd ever think that just plain food
Could stir up such a riot?
But open up the old 'fridge door
And suddenly it's *quiet.*

Jon Sebba
Red Winged Black Bird

ANNUAL CONTEST

Category 17 ~ Sci Fi / Fantasy Award

Sponsored by: Brick Cave Media

Judged by Jennifer Hernandez

Jennifer Hernandez serves as vice-president of the League of Minnesota Poets. Recent publications include *Sleet Magazine, Mom Egg Review, Halfway Down the Stairs*, and *Visual Verse*. Her work has been featured in several public installations: *The Clouds We Share* at Minnesota Center for Book Arts, the *Red Wing Poet/Artist Collaboration, Poetry in the Park in the Dark with Saint Paul Almanac, Detroit Lakes Flowerpot Poetry Walk, Nature Area Poetry Walk* in Richfield, and the *Mankato Poetry Walk and Ride*. She enjoys performing her poetry at readings both in person and online because the interaction between word and audience is where the magic happens.

Comin' Closer

It was big. Big as our house. Stomped
across the field, shook the barn walls.
Hiding wouldn't work. I just knew.

Screams stuck in my throat. Dad
snored heavy down the hall. Mom
flipped hash browns, and smiled as I
skittered into the kitchen.

"It's comin'," I yelled.

"Now Seth," Mom crooned,
patient-like. "Nothing out there."

"I saw it. Big, red sparks comin' out the
eyes. Spit leakin' out its mouth.
It just stepped over the chicken fence.
Grabbed two hens."

"Why the screamin' Seth?" Dad stumbled
into the kitchen, yanking on jeans. "Sit
down. Mom's settin' out breakfast."

I ate quick, then crept out to feed
the chickens. Sure didn't want to. Feathers
were stuck to great green globs of slime
on the path. Some stuck to my shoes.
I dropped the egg basket, tried to scrape
off the green goo. My hands got sticky.

Raced back to the house.

"Mom, Dad!" But no one answered.

Category 17: Sci-Fi / Fantasy Award
Second Place:Lisa Kamolnick ~ Blountville, Tennessee

True Story

I saw a fawn in the forest.
She flicked her tail, then in a flash
fled from the angry beast
at the edge of the enchanted woods.

Well …
that's not
exactly
true.

It wasn't really a forest
(or enchanted),
but that empty lot
down the street.

And the beast was just my dog,
Oliver, too busy chasing
a firefly to notice the fawn
paw and pace between trees.

The truth of the matter?

I was carried away—
by teensy forest fairies who inflame
my imagination, compel me
to tell stories, remind me

who I am. Maybe someday
I'll take flight with them, embrace
with delight a magical, mischievous
fairy-tale life. But not tonight.

I gently pull a leash, retract
my wings and dust a cul de sac,
tether my fairied feet to the pavement
of my suburban reality.

Interview with an Extraterrestrial

We have been visiting for millennia
as you can see in your human records
etched in stone, scribed on clay tablets,
told in stories around campfires.
Some of our kind stayed as observers
once we mastered shape-shifting, invisibility,
and, of course, a semblance of immortality;
our life spans far surpass humans'.

We are scientists who live and witness
all strata of human and non-human life;
you will find our legends everywhere,
even in your greater lakes and oceans.
You called us elf or fairy, dryad; named
us as gods, tricksters, and shape-shifters,
placed us in your stars to watch over you.
We appear supernatural and magical
to you who do not know advanced physics,
or the ways of energy manipulation.

We are here to ensure this solar system
will contain you for generations,
until your awkwardness, wars and violence
against one another is finally ended.
Those of us who have mastered star travel
must see your progress as non-threatening;
then we will be your doulas assisting your birth,
welcoming you to a universe barely imagined.
Or we will provide you hospice care.
This is your story to live
or not.

Kim Sosin
Sleeping Cranes

ANNUAL CONTEST

Category 18 ~ Shakespearean Award

Sponsored by: John Crawford

Judged by Judith Rycroft

Judith Rycroft has traveled the world, taught English, ESL, and Creative writing in many countries at high school and college level, and written poetry all her life. Many of her poems have appeared in various journals and magazines, and in the last four years she has published two books of poetry, *Colored Leaves* and *Perspectives*, both of which won the Oklahoma Writers Federation, Inc. annual award for Best Poetry Book. After retirement, Judith returned to Oklahoma to settle into old age with her dogs, Tai Chi, and poetry circles. She continues to write poetry; is working on her memoirs as a diplomat's wife, entitled *Thirty Years on the Verge of Diplomacy*; and loves to read her poetry aloud at every opportunity, believing that poetry sings the song of the soul and should be heard as well as read.

Category 18. Shakespearean Award
First Place: Linda Rittenhouse ~ Scottsdale, Arizona

Sockeye

'Neath topaz shafts of solar chandelier,
light sparkles off her iridescent gown
as liquid waltzes fill cool aqua sphere
and dancers on the pebbled floor press 'round.

She glides across admirer-studded room,
gets lost in languid orchestrated twirls.
To strains of Mother Nature's ancient tune,
shows belly trails of emerald, onyx pearls.

She chooses one to share his milky brew,
invites him to her hidden gravel grove
where life begins its circle dance anew
in urgent melding of each lifeforce trove.

Her gift of golden roe now gently spread,
her fate fulfilled; she rests her silver head.

Could I But...

Could I but greet the sun with freedom's grace,
burst forth with blissful spires of melody
still wrapped in afterglow of love's embrace,
proclaim my joy from tip of tulip tree!

Could I but lift proud beak to drink my fill
to fuel days' task of building gilded nest,
constructed with the finest twig and quill,
lined with soul's down from deep within my breast!

Could I but soar sweet thermal drafts 'til dawn--
not meet each dark a solo nightingale!
With tattered feather cape around him drawn,
who sings a tale of longing from his jail.

O! Spring me from this corner window cage!
'Fore I die choked on bitter tufts of rage!

The Sound of Bees In a Spring Apple Tree

There is a scent of promise in the air,
found rising shoulder high and heaven bound.
It brings me back to earth and plants me there,
both feet rooted mercifully in the ground.

I weed around the budding apple tree,
protecting all the nascent columbine;
hear every flower calling to each bee,
signaling nature's need to both align.

The door I might have entered is not closed,
but I am in no hurry to pass on.
The evening leaves me calmly predisposed
to listen for each buzz before they're gone.

When I have finished weeding, then I'll know
eternity's calling and I must go.

Kim Sosin
Nebraska Cardinal

ANNUAL CONTEST

Category 19 ~ TAPS Award

Sponsored by: Tucson Arts Poetry Series

Judged by Sam Rose Preminger

Sam Rose Preminger is a trans-nonbinary, Jewish writer and publisher. They hold an MFA from Pacific University, serve as editor-in-chief of NAILED Magazine, and are a co-founder of Lightship Press. Their poetry has previously appeared in *Prairie Schooner*, *North Dakota Quarterly*, *Michigan Quarterly Review*, *Narrative*, *Split Lip*, and *Yes Poetry*, among other publications. Their debut collections -- *'Cosmological Horizons'* and *'Our Streets'* -- were both published in 2022 by Kelsay Books and Lightship Press respectively. They live in Portland, OR with their partner and many house plants.

Pegasus

Artist depictions draw me in
to blue horses of Chagall, Franz Marc

where I'm nuzzled to the canvas,
painted into their stable.

I'm awed in the presence
of their live performance,

how each animal struts
and bows in a dressage

of two bodies, joining forces
with the rider in counted steps.

And in a race, both hearts beat
faster than the speed of breath,

harder than the wind-facing rain
now pelting skins, threatening

to slow their quickened pace,
but repelled by the sheen

of a black pearled creature
outstretched in gallop, hooved

to be in touch with earth,
winged to fly above it.

Mashed

Lemonade and bug bites—who cares?
We talk away the heat together
on the descending steps.

If you are a little insane
you are not the only one.

Let there be no more malaise
while we waste away the days
of crazy lazy summer.

Days unending blend beautifully
into the tangerine secrets of fall.

We disappear into our holes acting
like we've solved the world's problems.

Secretly driven by hunger we abscond
the front porch forum for supper.

Mom serves us mashed potato reality
that we slurp up like street cleaners
relentless in our humanity.

It's not enough

to inscribe graffiti on walls
        dripping with rainy paint, blotching
        a trail on the sidewalk, just across
        the street from where you grew up
        suffering in your newness

or to absorb bullets of incoming
        heartache, dead saplings on the median,
        a young man standing over them,
        too much of Dallas, Columbine, Sandy Hook
        or tallying Facebook friends
        ghosted in a pill bottle, the hole
        in a boat to slake an underwater thirst

and still not enough to document what no longer
        lives in pictures, photos of Polaroid heaven
        without negatives – all smiles, splashes
        at arm's length and farther, souvenirs
        of a future tense marking time until
        a final line evolves from the end of this one,
        to be the elegy for those
        who cannot say enough

Kim Sosin
Green Heron

ANNUAL CONTEST

Category 20 ~ Traditional Rhyme Award

Sponsored by Betsy Clark

Judged by Jeff Price

Jeff Price is now in his thirty-second year teaching English, the past twenty-three at Science Hill High School in Johnson City, Tennessee. He just completed thirty-eight years coaching wrestling on the high school, college, and middle school levels, a career which earned him a spot in the Tennessee Chapter of the National Wrestling Hall of Fame. He resides in Johnson City with his wife Julie, as well as a trio of cats - Merlyn, Mister, and Cleo, and his boon companion, Dewman "Buddy" Doggs, the rescue dog who rescued him. Last summer he decided to try to get some of his work published. His poem *Falcon Dreaming* appears in the 2022 *James Dickey Review*; his first collection of poems, *One Steady Glance*, was released by Redhawk Publications last April. It is available through the Redhawk Publications website, Amazon, Barnes and Noble, or by contacting the author directly at wartopper@gmail. com.

Category 20: Traditional Rhyme Award – Shakespearean Sonnet
First Place: Linda Rittenhouse ~ Scottsdale, Arizona

Conspiracy

If hearts are merely metronomes in rhyme,
smooth ventricles in perfect harmony,
why did mine stumble, erase ticks of time
with every duet's beat I sang with thee?

If minds are moved by puppet master hands
controlling mundane mortal marionettes,
why does mine carry on this phantom dance
with broken strings of circular regrets?

If souls are solely remnants of a past,
assembled trails of chosen memories,
why is mine like a whirlpool clogged with sand
that spirals to hell-bound eternity?

Why do the three conspire to love you still?
O! How they mock the strength of human will!

Category 20: Traditional Rhyme Award
Second Place: Linda R. Payne ~ Ramsey, Minnesota

Kokopelli Play Your Flute
a kyrielle

O, Kokopelli play your flute
with magic notes so warm and sweet
to chase away this wintry brute.
Please bring back spring on winged feet.

Your face appears upon the moon
with full-blown smile, aglow, upbeat.
So, play for us a joyful tune;
please bring back spring on winged feet!

Fair spirit of fertility
upon your back you carry seeds
a symbol of fecundity.
Please, bring back spring on winged feet.

O, music spirit how we long
for winter's cold to now retreat,
to hear your blissful, mirthful song.
Please! Bring back spring on winged feet!

Unvanquished

Sleep tight precious villain,
stopped cold in your tracks,
clad in warm jammies and
cloak of pitch black.

Around you lies chaos:
a jumble of toys,
sticks, rocks, dead insects—
prized loot of small boys.

Your light saber glows,
minacious and steady.
No rival dare threaten
with it at the ready.

All day you battled
to stave off defeat
from those who would tame you
and halt your swift feet.

You conquered fierce foes,
mighty in number.
But one proved relentless—
you succumbed to sweet slumber.

This isn't surrender,
just transient retreat,
an unwelcome respite
in the haven of sleep.

Gail Denham
Yellow Poppy Wagon Wheel

ANNUAL CONTEST

Category 21 ~ Western Theme Award

Sponsored by Stuart Watkins

Judged by Amanda Marie Gipson

Amanda Marie Gipson is a creative writer with a decade of expe-
rience in community-based agricultural education. She earned an MFA
from Wilkes University in June of 2023, where she served as the Coordi-
nator of the Writing Center. Her place-based writing is often inspired
by time at M. Agr at Colorado State University and centers a deep appre-
ciation for the American West in all its diversity and complexity. A
grown-up horse girl, she currently serves as the Fiction Editor
for *Northern Appalachia Review.*

Cowboy Days

Dawn greets me
With a kiss
As I wake
To a busy day,
Three hundred head
Of cattle
Must be moved
To a higher pasture
Before the rains.
With only five of us
To drive them,
We'll be earning
Our pay.
The horses will be
As worn out as we
When Eve finally
Calls us in for supper,
Stew for us
And hay for them,
We won't suffer,
But it will be a tough
Task to conquer.

Burro Creek

Arizona deserts, broken by asphalt,
mining, and isolated ranches that cling
to the edge of a hard way to live,
still have wild places, unwalked by men.
The heat consumes water, animals,
plants and cracks bare rock,
swirls up wind devils full
of leaves, tiny pebbles and dust.
Speeding on State Road 93
north of Wickenburg, south of Wikiup,
a driver could miss fragile beauty,
dismiss the parched blurs
until Burro Creek's high rocky canyon
catches you in its afternoon reds,
the curved white concrete bridge
a testament to an unknown engineer.
This mini-Grand Canyon holds secrets,
invisible herds of wild burros,
and more than a few scoured skeletons.
The tiny creek far below, winding down
from Santa Maria Range, is wisped away
except for the barest trickle
through sand and jasper. Echoes
from the call of a hawk spiraling
on the rising thermals
bounce from the red canyon.

Contests

"Sheriff, Sheriff, come quick -
she's at it again!

"The metaphors have been rounded up.
She's working the stray similes.

The iambs are already in a pentameter,
now syllables have scattered all over the range.
Didn't see a single rhyme.

"I think they're fixin' to be loaded up
and sent to the National Poetry Society.
You gotta help!"

"Hell, boy. I ain't messing with no
pistol-packing poet. Just don't say
nothin' and lay low. It'll be over in March.

Kim Sosin
Rose Breasted Finch

ANNUAL CONTEST

Category 22 ~ Wild Places, Open Spaces Award

Sponsored by Steve Chaffee

Judged by Susan McMillan

Susan McMillan is a retired freelance writer and editor. Her poetry has appeared in many anthologies and journals, most recently *Talking Stick, Deep Wild—Writing from the Backcountry*, and *Oakwood*. She has participated in the Cracked Walnut literary reading series, is a Maria W. Faust Sonnet Contest regional award recipient, a senior editor for RockPaperPoem, and co-creator of two Bright Light Stories in the *Night* e-chapbooks. She served as poet laureate for the city of Rochester, Minnesota from 2019-23 by engaging the community and creating opportunities for poets through collaborative projects, events, and learning opportunities. She is a longtime member of the League of Minnesota Poets.

Category 22: Wild Places, Open Spaces Award
First Place: Paul Buchheit ~ Chicago, Illinois

First Ride on the Transcontinental Railroad

It's spring of '69, I'm heading west
to California. Great Sierra peaks
confront the locomotive, pistons pressed
against relentless heights. The cabin reeks
from blackish fumes, the roaring engines strain
to muscle up the slope. But paradise
is suddenly below us as the train
relaxes: mighty rivers seem to splice
majestic hills with swaths of greenery.
And now, with sparks above its shrieking wheels
the train descends, and we are falling free
with frightful speed, until the crazed appeals
for mercy all around me turn to calm
amidst a gentle valley's airy balm.

Category 22: Wild Places, Open Spaces Award
Second Place: Dianne Brown ~ Wellton, Arizona

Kofa Mountain Sorcery

Miles of spikey broken
teeth, stony fingers—my own
bony hand—point to
megalithic castles
high on sheer cliffs
nary a toe-hold for
dream-catching
lizards

Narrow table rocks set
with granite cloths
candelabra—wall shadows
flickering in sunlight
primitive fire dances to
long-gone sky gods

No rest for hungry eyes
to count or fathom the
spiraled glyphs tattooed
on every limb

What are you saying
Kofa sisters, to this
hungry spirit? Fill
me with your secret
incantations, draw me
into the circle, and show
me, what the years added
to your baskets of
uncertain fruit

I want your ancient
spells birthed in this
unpeopled land
pressed into
my bare
uninitiated
hands

The Sierra Nevada's Range of Light

Dedicated to John Muir

Mother Nature spreads her enthusiasm like a child.
Transforming energy into life, she moves
the elements by cataclysmic fire, ice and flood,
easing ancient glaciers down mountain chasms,
like a poet melding metaphors.

She enriches the soil, sows and nourishes,
like a master gardener tending every bud.
Wind and rain, the chipmunks,
birds and squirrels, the worms-
each elemental member of her clan
work together in constant harmony,
spreading seeds, sprouting dogwoods,
pines, berries, wild roses and sunflowers.
She fills each fluted rift with gems
and distills every essence of travertine,
granite crags, geysers, pools and gayest plumes-
like van Gogh, bidding his brush from the palette.

You too can flush the heart and find
the harmony of a thousand whisperings
that call, plead and shift the transient muted life
man vaguely calls his own.
Let nature introduce you to her rhythmic dance
of glacial ice, of streams and waterfalls,
flesh and wood and rocky sepulchers.
Share this wondrous dwelling place with angels-
this wide expanse of land and lakes;
these mountains with their ebullient streams
filled with life and curiosity, in finite form,
are infinitely heaven!

The sun is in the west and setting low,
chasing shadows and scrubbing every peak
with the divine light of alpenglow.

YOUTH CONTEST

Honorable Mentions
(In rank order ~ 1HM, 2HM, 3HM, 4HM)

Youth Grades 1-4
Venaya Arvizu from John E. White Elementary, Tucson ~
  Shoelaces
Isaiah Knight Jillela from Legacy Online Academy, Chandler ~
  Poem, Poem, Where Are You Hiding?
Yoonseo Cho from CTA Independence Campus, Chandler ~
  Shine
Mackenzie Darimont from Leman Academy, Oro Valley ~
  What can a cat do?
Aeneas C. Pedrego from Homeschool, Green Valley ~
  The Quarterback

Youth Grades 5-8
Gracie Moore from American Leadership Academy, Gilbert ~
  My Garden
Redwan Hossain from Legacy Traditional School, Laveen Village ~
  Ode to the Axolotls
Natalie Leuschner from Glendale Preparatory Academy, Glendale ~
  A Day in the Life of a Doorknob
Isabella Goodall from Esperero Canyon Middle School, Tucson ~
  As I See Me
Daphney Gomez from Alice Byrne Elementary, Yuma ~
  A Way of Life
Itzelany Rivas from Alice Byrne Elementary, Yuma ~
  Little Monsters

Youth Grades 9-12
Damari Campos from Lake Havasu High School, Lake Havasu ~
  But All that I am is You
Avalynn Strickland from Intelli High School, Glendale ~
  If quiet was a sound
Kim Mungia from Mica Mountain High School, Tucson ~
  Worthy
Cruz Martinez from Phoenix College Preparatory Academy, Phoenix ~
  Arizona
Violet Hilderbrand from Marana High School, Marana ~
  My Country

ANNUAL CONTEST

Honorable Mentions
(In rank order ~ 1HM, 2HM, 3HM, 4HM)

Category 1: ASPS Award
Linda LaVere Hatch ~ *Sister to Brother*
Michele Worthington ~ *Sleeping in the Anthropocene*
Stephen Bochinski ~ *Riding Through the Night*

Category 2: Aging Award
Brenda Wildrick ~ *Long Silver Hair Dancing with the Wind*
CChristy White ~ *Each Day I Forget Something*
Dawn Loeffler ~ *I Can't Drive 55*

Category 3: Ekphrastic Award
Laura Hansen ~ *Le Donne Val D'Orcia*
Terry Jude Miller ~ *Bringing in the Maple Sugar*
Janet McMillan Rives ~ *Across*

Category 4: Our Changing Environment Award
Martha H. Balph ~ *An Inconvenient Truth*
Jonathan Bennett ~ *Resignation*
Charles Firmage ~ *On Our Way to Oz*

Category 5: Five C's of Arizona Award
Jane Randall ~ *Inflation at the Fabric Store*
Jerri Hardesty ~ *A Place for Simplicity*
Janet McMillan Rives ~ *Whitehouse Canyon*

Category 6: Gardening Award
Cate Gable ~ *Apples in a Time of Plague*
Gene Twaronite ~ *Attitude*
CChristy White ~ *Unky Bunk's Garden*
Henry A. Childers ~ *Common Ground*

Category 7: Haiku Award
Mark Hammerschik ~ *In Situ*
Martha H. Balph ~ *western tanager*
Donna Geise ~ *Admiring the hawk*

ANNUAL CONTEST

Honorable Mentions
(In rank order ~ 1HM, 2HM, 3HM, 4HM)

Category 8: Humor Award
Alan Perry ~ *Dropped Calls*
Henry A. Childers ~ *Overheard While Jogging*
Trina Lee ~ *Star Party*

Category 9: Jesse Belle Rittenhouse Memorial Award
Beverly Stanislawski ~ *Neon Dreams*
Daniel B. Pickett ~ *In Yonder Dreams*
Laura Rodley ~ *Sudden Snow*

Category 10: Legacy Award
Henry A. Childers ~ *Nothing to Say*
Alan Perry ~ *Obituary for a House*
Henry A. Childers ~ *The Radio*

Category 11: Native Lands and Voices Award
Lorraine Jeffery ~ *The Import of a Metaphor*
Donna Isaac ~ *Highway 88*
CChristy White ~ *Bone Flowers*

Category 12: Nature's Metaphor Award
Linda Rittenhouse ~ *Canyon*
Wyatt Welch ~ *Gate's Pass, Tucson*
Anita Dees ~ *Inside the Crystal Cavern*

Category 13: Previously Published Poem Award
Alan Perry ~ *Reflection*
Martha H. Balph ~ *Adam's Hand*
Alan Perry ~ *Encroachment*
Rex Arrasmith ~ *Jesus Meets Eve on Ascension Day*

Category 14: Previously Rejected Poem Award
Michael Spears ~ *Chewing Gum*
Betty Jo Middleton ~ *I've Got Mail*
Daniel J. Fitzgerald ~ *Incense*

Category 15: Prose Poem Award
Charles Firmage ~ *Zebras*
Richard Ramsey ~ *What Would His Face Say*

Category 16: Rhyming Poem for Children Award
Donna Isaac ~ *The Dragon Shares His Truth*
Delores (Dee Dee) Chumley ~ *Cow Chow Café*
Cate Gable ~ *It's Time*

Category 17: Sci / Fi Fantasy Award
Terry Jude Miller ~ *the last computer*
Joyce Kohler ~ *An Abecedarian Homage to the Artist James C. Christensen*
Jerri Hardesty ~ *Blind Date*

Category 18: Shakespearean Award
Paul Buchheit ~ *Seduction on a Morning Walk*
Daniel Moreschi ~ *Ephemeral Shrouds*
Joyce Kohler ~ *Old Apples*

Category 19: TAPS Award
David Navarro ~ *I Dance Amazing There*
Michele Worthington ~ *Morning Paper*
David Navarro ~ *Launch Window Looms*

Category 20: Traditional Rhyme Award
Gurupreet K. Khalsa ~ *Flying by White Cliffs*
Laura Rodley ~ *Headwaters*
Martha H. Balph ~ *Genesis*

Category 21: Western Theme Award
Crystie Cook ~ *How the Sunset Listens*
Terry Jude Miller ~ *cinched*
Laura Rodley ~ *Burro*

Category 22: Wild Places, Open Spaces Award
Joyce Kohler ~ *Sargassum-of-the-Sea*
Jean Varda ~ *Summit Lake*
Beverly Stanislawski ~ *Nature's Night Performance*

Jon Sebba
Black Crested Night Heron

Member Poems

The hallmark of the Arizona State Poetry Society is our annual anthology *Sandcutters*. First published in 1967, it included winning poems from the membership in three categories in 12 monthly contests. Some years later, *Sandcutters* grew to include an Annual Contest open to all poets in the world with cash awards given to the top three winners in each category.

Today, *Sandcutters* has expanded to include:
- An invitation to the Featured Speaker(s) poet(s) at the 2024 ASPS Conference in January to submit a poem of their choice;
- Winning poems of the top three winners in our Member Contests held five times a year;
- Winning poems of the top three winners in our occasional Special Member Contest (based on a theme);
- Winning poems of the top three winners in each category of the Annual Contest;
- Winning poems of the top three winners in our annual Youth Contest in three grade groupings;
- An invitation to ASPS members who have not submitted and/or won in any of the contests, to submit one poem of their choice for inclusion in *Sandcutters*; and
- Featured visual art submitted by our members and chosen by the Co-Editors.

The Board of Directors is pleased to include the Member Poem section in *Sandcutters* as our way of highlighting the varied talents of our Members, and to thank them for their loyalty in supporting the Arizona State Poetry Society.

The Board extends a sincere thank you to all those who sponsored the Annual Contest categories, which allowed for the cash awards.

Carol Baxter ~ Pine, Arizona

Messages To My Ex

My mac and cheese is runny.
I still lack your precision.
But we were newly married then

always broke
she didn't fix us.

Her four-year innocent voice unwavering,
(How is her struggle to understand so complete?)
　　"Can you please send,
　　My Daddy, your friend,
　　a letter?"
A shorter number of months
then ever I'd have believed,
to discover I don't need you,
to discover you don't miss me.

Our little mimic misses you
with a big heart all her own.
Although it's an open visitation,
there's five hundred miles
between her homes.

Far away in L.A.
check your messages
ya gotta smile:
　　"Thank you for the gum.
　　Happy Halloween.
　　Can you call me in the morning
　　after you do your sit-ups,
　　and your chin-ups?"
My morning routine has changed,
while yours remains the same.

I can program the TV now.
Mechanics can't fool me.
You can't bring me to tears any more,
yet she brings me to my knees.
　"Mommy, I love you."

Gary Bowers ~ Phoenix, Arizona

blue moon

backlit trio on the bri**m**
lifted yond the con & pr**o**
unseen force I G N I T E S and L**o**
extra luminescent: L i m **n**

David Boyce ~ Ogden, Utah

Jesus, He Wears the Stain so Well

Jesus, He wears the stain so well
Having hung on the cross.
He bridged the gap twixt
Heaven and hell,
And gained where all was lost.

Our Lord commanded tombs release
Bodies they once have stored.
All will awake from endless sleep,
And live forever more.

Cancer won't sting, nor eye will cry
Tears gushed at Heaven's door.
All tears of pain b'come tears of joy
As angels leap and soar.

Meanwhile, we'll wait with broken hearts
As we do hope to see
Loved ones ascend to glorious heights
Where in Thy Bosom be.

Reference to Bernard of Clairvaux, et al.

Marilyn Brodhurst ~ Tucson, Arizona

My Mother's Legacy

Under the dim light of the lamp
The needles echo the metronome
Of our lives…
Click…click…click

Quick flicks of the wrist defy definition
 As the pattern emerges from secret memory,
Teller of dreams
        (when you grow up)
Keeper of past
        (when I was young).

Sweaters designed to hold heart and warmth,
Hats and mittens for fun in the snow
        (play while you can)
Slippers with pom-poms and argyle socks
        (walk straight and true)
Strands tying family in motherly love.

Pointed needles lie,
Silent and still
In balls of woolen threads
Guarding a legacy of life.

Steve Chaffee ~ Green Valley, Arizona

My Prima Ballerina

nestled near a tinkling brook
adorned with moss and lichen encrusted boulders
and sprays of bracken fern

she sports canary sized buds, yellow petals,
yellow pointed sepals and yellow trailing spurs
like a heavenly comet
a shooting star
she shakes, she shouts
demands my rapt attention

she twirls in the breeze
on long slender stems
my prima ballerina
floating on air
prancing, dancing
she knows she's beautiful
flaunts her saucy attitude, her femininity
perfectly appointed
yellow columbine
hearten and surprise

Mariposa Crossing

Pushing against the dirty
chipped white turn style
Mexican shoppers from Nogales line up looking for bargains on the
American side.
An American doctor to the poor in jeans and sneakers waits then
steps forward.
"Get back" yells the border guard,
canister of mace hanging from her vest,
H&K double action pistol tipped slightly forward on her belt.
He backs up and rolls his eyes.
She flashes him a hot stare.
"What's so damn funny," she says in her hard Rosie Perez, Alien II, New
York City Puerto Rican accent.
"That's a sign of insubordination. I've got to stand here all day in this
heat and put up with your disrespect?"
The doctor lowers his head and waits.
She motions him forward, scrutinizes his passport and thrusts it back.
He clears the border and travels across time and the history of two nations
into Arizona streets lined with discounted clothing shops.
The doctor glances back at the border wall,
shakes his head,
and smiles sadly.

Suzanne Jacobson Cherry ~ Mesa, Arizona

Desert Voices

How do I speak
Of the voices on the wind?
The ancient songs of those who
Have gone before call to me
In languages unknown
They tell tales of civilizations
Long past and forgotten
People whose faces we see
In our dreams, who
Crave understanding

It is in the desert among
The memories of the winds
Where the voices call to me
My feet grow roots in the sand
And find anchor in the hard caliche
Which defies the defiling penetration
Of shovel and pick, refusing to submit
To the ravages of human progress
Those who have been here before
Moved on with the advance of time,
Leaving nothing behind but
Scattered sherds of their living
And of their dying

Their creative expressions
Of life in this hard-earned world
Are lost, there is nothing left
Of their blood and their bones,
But the ancient voices
That call to we who stand,
Eyes closed, minds attuned
To the call of another time,
Another world,
Not really gone but simply
Beyond the Veil
Between this world
And the one beside

John W. Crawford ~ Arkadelphia, Arkansas

Easter Is the Best

The springtime Easter season I like best.
The cool, fresh air inspires my very soul.
The flowering bulbs of pink and all the rest
Lift me up high and make me feel so whole.

The gorgeous shades of green seem to abound --
From light to dark and all hues in between --
And robins chirp with sweet songs all around.
The combination makes my spirit keen.

Some say that nothing beats the Christmas night -That joy of life is ever
in the air --
But from the Easter season I find sight
Of hopes and dreams that cause us all to share.

Oh, winter, how you always seem to fade
When followed by the Spring and Easter shade.

Hank Dallago ~ Tucson, Arizona

The Clay Vessel

Hands
hold
clay
close
benign
to century
aged sediment:
shapes wide base
adds long thin walls
broad furrowed mouth
as a swan bending her neck
skyward to receive fresh rain
single pores imbued with life
offers herself, a receptacle to
rejuvenate a child's thirst
revive a dried flower
quench prisoner's
first prayer.

Stephanie DuPont ~ Sugar Hills, Georgia

Moss-clad Memories

The autumn evening dims the grounds—
A faded brick surrounds derelict,
Decrepit gardens, rotted, gnarly roots.
Within the walls—
I am the ruin, not yet neglected.
Sometimes I am the stones, but other times—
I am as fragile as the moss-filled grass,
With bones that break under the weight of ivy vines,
Entangling, strangling time—
Whether or not I water them.
I spritz the stones to watch them slowly grow—
Decay—disintegrate and die—
Alive—the earth grows silent, light then fades,
Another day is withering away.
We are all walking ghosts;
We, like the ruins, meet our silent end.
What will we build before we are the remnants?

Stephen Fierro ~ Tucson, Arizona

Ode to the donor

Can't Explain

My grief comes in waves, flooded by my tears
Lonely came the days altered by my fears
Gone by are the years honored memories saved
Softer are the tears sweeter dreams now craved
Dreams of days gone by before changes came
Reasons that we cry sorrows stay the same
Time may ease the pain fast it will fly
No one can explain still can't answer why

Loss feels so strong sometimes minds go blank
How one day went wrong the day our heart sank
Caring friends we thank given great support
Hugs I highly rank death notes still to sort
Red Cross sends report thanks to the donor
Time now to abort tears of this mourner
Organs Red Cross claim questions why we die
No one can explain still can't answer why

Heart that still beats, lungs that breathe again
It's life that some seek stranger or a friend
Proof that doctor's send complete use of skin
Natural ways to blend everyone will win
Red Cross will recall those that now live on
Gifts for those who fall makes a life time bond
Many still remain many will apply
No one can explain still can't answer why

To us he is gone others will sing along
His life in a song making others strong
On the donor train a soul that can fly
Still we can't explain there's no answer why

Anita Fonte ~ Tucson, Arizona

Geoffrey Beene's Scenes at the Museum

I.
Oh, girl, you twirl
with joy and balance.
You jive and keep alive
the spirit of:
"just because I want to!"

II.
An arabesque
does it best
to show the lace
and frame the face
in netting black
and dramatic dance.

III.
My mother lov'd
"Ric Rack" trim.
She sewed it
on our blouses;
it fell into flounces
and pleats of our skirts,
tumbling over petticoats,
my sister,
and me.

Shari Crane Fox ~ San Jose, California

Fantasy #2009

In some other universe—I killed my first
husband. I live near the ocean, and at
night I listen to the hiss of the waves losing
their grip and the just barely discernible
sound of the sand, softly laughing.

Roberta Gale ~ Tucson, Arizona

That Time My Neighbor Ran over a Rattlesnake

Some make sport
of swerving toward her diamonds
triangular head, forked tongue in/out darting
dancing with desert partner.

And then she is the dance floor
skin slug-soft until sea-horsed by heat
a cowboy boot in the middle of the road.

Once, dust marked her sandy trails
to her asphalt evening resting place
its radiating heat now her grave.

Once, in cotton candy weeds
she waited, polite and silent
for mice, lizards, pack rats, rabbits.

A good girl at a recital until her turn to feed
she venomed with the rapidity of the roadrunner
she could take if she chose.

Rattling only when her crib was threatened
striking only when struck or stepped on
she could, would kill.

Now her milk could, would, save no one
just spilled monsoon tears/just one more nuisance
gone on this tar-black desert road.

Paula Goldsmith ~ Mesa, Arizona

Have You Ever Seen?

Have you ever seen a sunrise
that took your breath away?
Have you ever seen a sunset that was
very magical?
Have you ever seen a baby smile?
Have you ever seen beautiful blue water
hit the shore?
Then you have seen the smile of God.

Marlana-Patrice Pugh Hamer ~ San Tan Valley, Arizona

True Romance

Weeds
swear God is laughing.
Testing and tempting us with our own sweat
before shadows rise with suns.
Others say you are verdant reminders of the shame
that absorbs our church rays.
Seducing even   beetles and hummingbirds.
Lilacs are also your fools
and every other living creature who wishes
to sway
with you all day
in winds   unsupervised by parents.
No mothers assigning you chores
or fathers warning us to stay in yards.
Crisscrossing sacred pavements   and boundaries.

Weeds,
we clear, burn, and forgive you.
A trash day trinity.
Yet you   disrespect,   defy logic   by multiplying the next day.
Then the next   and the next.
Invading sidewalk cracks, parking lots,   and frontal lobes!
Pricking fingers   with raw pleasure.
Spoiling   our Sunday Best forever!
We loathe   and adore you,

WEEDS!

Mark Hammerschick ~ Highland Park, Illinois

Expanding Eyes

Where do dreams go on vacation?
Do they take a plane a train or the subway
as they look for places to stay
on the edge of infinite light
knocking about like a bunch of leptons and quarks
lost in the labyrinth of dimensional longitude.

Quantum quandary
galactical scope
observing the observer tips the scales
toward anti-matter
caught in the coagulated corner
of your quasar eyes
expanding silently into forever.

Aaron Holst ~ Sheridan, Wyoming

Autumn
(haiku sonnet)

Colorado spruce
defiant in strong wind gusts
needles and cones fly

overnight wind slows
aspen rustles brittle leaves
quaking in cold air

wearing ermine coat
grass sparkles in morning sun
first autumn diamonds

summer chores undone
hidden green serpent hose lies
in snow covered lawn

changing seasons turning from

Frank Iosue ~ Oro Valley, Arizona

Titanica

There is only one voyage:
Toward myth. Toward tragedy.

Dismantled on the bottom are
the fragile totalities.

The wonder
of worlds broken
to their final bits.

In the blackness,
every being
is a light being
torn asunder,

with its little trappings
and assembly of objects
hiding in that
illumination.

A scream rises.
A ghost of
the one unraveling.

The last reality,
the severing of small things,

now, in the night,
finally prepared
for the unsought engagement,

the dark and privileged
descent.

Kaya Kotzen ~ Scottsdale, Arizona

Growing into Knowing
Inspired by Mary Oliver's poem, The Journey

One day you finally knew that you didn't know anything,
even yourself, that you trusted too much in others.
Your own urges were but a whisper you could not hardly hear.

One day you finally knew that it was time to wake up,
time to say hello to your own heart and tend it,
time to stop pleasing others and learn to please yourself.

One day you finally knew you could set your own path in the world
even if you made mistakes and had detours along the way,
You knew you could live with yourself better if you trusted
what was real for you, regardless of whether it was a fear,
a doubt, or a knowing of which way to go,

One day you finally knew you had to claim your own life.
You had to learn to lean into the unknown, even when you blew it.
There were lessons to learn and challenges that made you stronger.
Each one grew you, made you more resilient
and a little less afraid.
Sometimes it was just all about taking baby steps,
instead of leaps and bounds and you learned that was ok.
You began to trust your pace, your inner nudges, and whatever
showed up for you on the path.

On day you finally knew that you had grown into yourself,
trusted your own likes and dislikes and the friends you made who
accepted you for who you were, not who they wanted you to be.
You just finally got tired of not knowing and you opened your heart
and your life began to lead you to what you needed, though it was not
always what you wanted.
Life became more real, more vibrant, more everything, as you began
to trust yourself. Inner wisdom came with life experience
and that knowing, that inner wisdom, was the truest thing of all.

Sandra Luber ~ Tucson, Arizona

Betwixt

Mind has a monstrous mouth
she eats you up with memory
swept by breathless stories
destructive impatience, haste,
an absolute refusal to live in the NOW
or even be aware of its fragrance.
Mind guesses with expectation
at an unknown future
as if she had the gift of knowing
rather than living with curiosity.

Sometimes, when the interior light glows
I have witnessed her
smash through a gate, uninvited,
yet always welcome as timeless.
She lays like a sleepy cat
hangs out in the gaps
between leaping words
phrases set apart by
ellipses, commas, spaces, periods.

Now, she steps aside
the world splinters off
and silence rests at home
placeholder of the sacred.

William Moody ~ Tucson Arizona

View Out the Window

I have looked out the window
hundreds of times
without seeing, but today I saw.
Before me posed a tranquil scene
far from the hectic jumble of life.

A boat moored at the dock
on the placid lake waters
highlighted in the soft morning light,
beyond the glass, framed
with two tall ponderosa trees.

Dark reflections from the trees
on the far shore finished the
outline of this irenic moment.
I could recognize the brush strokes
of a Winslow Homer painting.

In the green boat, a wooden oar
casually rested on wooden seats
awaiting the rower's grasp.
Not a whorl, nor a wave disturbed
the peaceful lake surface.

Gone was the normal bedlam of nature —
a breeze rustling the tree branches,
silvery trout rising to feed
leaving circular ripples in the water,
swallows swooping, darting, feeding.

The rhythms of nature
taking a brief respite,
no chaos to disturb the
sweet sounds of harmony —
calming, motionless.

This simplified composition stirred
my heart, I too felt at peace.
By taking the time to pause, to see —
I could touch the earth, smell the forest
and lake, breathe the morning air.

Daniel Moreschi ~ Wales, United Kingdom

A Vernal Vision

Where branches are bridges and sedges are screens
and waters reflect a celestial shine,
the earth is a canvas so seeds become means
to make a terrain of Edenic design.

This scrupulous labor attentively lays
the pedestals of an herbaceous surround:
a savorous haven that settles and sways
once nectars and milkweeds emerge from the ground.

Within the embraces of petals and blades,
arrangements of delicate gemstones are drawn.
They cluster with luster while under the shades
and wait for the livening ardor of dawn.

These satiny structures then break from within.
A subtle subsidence exposes their cores,
while shimmers embellish the layers of skin
of ravenous larvae that rise from the pores:

a subtle invasion embodied in slinks,
that fashion a hole in each folial hold,
before manifesting, with sinewy links,
the tenuous tents of a nebulous mold.

Away from the host plants, a cycle of peaks
blossoms on beds with a billowy blend;
a bounty of fragrance with succulent streaks
that beckons the chrysalis slumbers to end.

The butterflies waken and gently undo
the remnants and binds of their previous form.
They cling while their flickering wingspans accrue
and hie to the heights like an opaline swarm.

They fluidly frolic. They run on the breeze.
They brighten the glow of the greenery's gleam.
They tend to each stem. They encircle the trees;
They nourish and flourish, and kindle a dream.

213

Edidtsa Perillo ~ Green Valley, Arizona

First Desert Holiday

The Antique globe twinkles,
"Snow" is blanketing the small plaza inside.
She watches it, full of longing.
    Ready, *love*?
Her partner asks, their coats in hand.
She looks up, sighing,
    Yes, *dear*.
They smile knowingly, even as she looks back down,
    You don't want to be late, *love*.
She nods and swaddles herself in the warm coat,
They head out hand in hand.
As they drive up...
    Are we at the light show?
She stares excitedly at the sign,
They offer their arm, like an old-world gentleman,
    Let's get some coco, they offer.
They sip while strolling through the magically lit archways,
    This is so *beautiful*.
    Yes, *you are*, they say to themselves.
    Love, come see this!
They relock arms and wander through the tunnel.
After some lovely moments later, the tunnel opens to a sparkling plaza.
Couples flow on the dance floor along with the music in the crisp air,
As the fake snow floats around them as they dance.
    Darling, she gasps.
    Merry Christmas, my *love*.
She smiles and pulls them into the flowing magic of the plaza,
As they spin her into themselves they share a passionate kiss.
But something wet touches both their faces,
They look up, *snow*.
Real snow is falling in the desert.

D'Anne Pientka ~ Phoenix, Arizona

a drink of life

alcoholic years
      welcoming death
until it comes near
      too near
now fighting for life
      too late

JamesRobert Platt ~ Tempe, Arizona

In Heaven's Eye
with fond remembrance

Mourn ye not for me
              my friends
    For certain
          we shall meet again

Though time be short
             upon this earth
    In Heaven's eye
          we prove our worth

For God has no doubts
             about me
    I've traveled
          in good company

With family true
             and words true straight
    I'll wait for ye
          by Peter's Gate

Elaine A. Powers ~ Tucson, Arizona

Pelican Grief

I needed to find the small pelican statue
A sentinel for decades
Only slightly pink, not flashy,
Watching Mom's departures and greeting her returns

Her last house, furnished with Florida décor
Comfortable for two, especially roomy for one
Until the day the Gulf of Mexico came within
Possessions tossed and tumbled
Furniture floated and swirled
Jumbled like seashells left in the high tide's wake

In the muck that remained
I sought the symbol of my mother
I wanted the pelican to come with me
To share my Arizona home as my mom had
Before she died
So, I searched

Mom wasn't there in the overturned couch
Or in the pieces of the lamps
Under the legless tables
Behind the crushed TV
Impaled by a bookshelf

Beside the detached steps
Lay the little pelican
Decapitated
A sign from Mom to move on

My memories of Mom are safe and dry
Only my future in her house
Dissolved

Walter Ralston ~ Hyannis, Massachusetts

Unfenced

A fellow poet has encouraged me
to experiment with writing in discrete,
defined forms. As with most of my pieces,
free form is my preference.

I have written a number of haikus, sensing,
experiencing the form as an angry sieve
for my heart's expression. While I may have
missed some understanding of haikus, I
am left with the feeling that this form is
a gauntlet thrown down, daring the reader
to discover the connection among
three lines. It becomes a challenge
of the intellect, any emotion
encountered to be filtered out.

In poetry, I feel that it is
the reader's experience that
is paramount. What does your
heart have to say? Not 'how are
these lines connected?'

Besides, it just may be that I prefer
a less disciplined, less constrained
mode of expression. Who cares what
the box looks like anyway? Rip it
open. Let's see what's inside!

Mark Redfearn ~ Temecula, California

Hung with Flowers

Hung with flowers is the plum—
Surely fruitful times will come!
Blossoms hung along the bough
Are the plum tree's solemn vow
That when blooming days are done,
Fruits will ripen one by one—
One by one along the bough,
Where white blossoms open now.

Jody Serey ~ Glendale, Arizona

mixed marriage, 1990

in Big Stone at the café
she had made him breakfast
her eyes too tired for ten o'clock
it took him days to mention college
or the tennis racket in his car
she had touched his sleeping bag
with fingers asking questions
but made no comment on his boots that
waited, empty, like locust shells

they bought the license in the spring,
then stopped to tell her mother
his parents sent a check, which he
drove a hundred miles to cash,
and copies of prescriptions

he learned to drop his eyes, and
fish in silence on the river
his adjusted grip could field-gut rabbits
or wrap around the ax
her brothers claimed him when the evenings
echoed crickets, and the moon was blue
she'd see him disappear
with the bottle and the men

Kim McNealy Sosin ~ Omaha, Nebraska

Lonely: a Senryu Triptych

never thought you'd stay
gossamer wings never do
each moonrise a gift

thunder bursts wake me
rainfall batters the window
the front door slams shut

listen to the night
beyond the gray mourning doves
they murmur you you

Joy Valerius ~ Tucson, Arizona

I Never Throw Out my Old Shoes

no matter how many
miles they have seen.

Is it my way of holding on to
the places they have gone

or am I simply a hoarder
unwilling to let them go?

I think maybe this pair
I will use for doing yard work,

another I will wear
out in the rain.

Year after year they pile up
on my closet floor, some

piled high up on a shelf
above where I hang up my clothes.

Boxes and boxes of shoes
tumbling out

every time I open
the door.

what scenery do they hope
to see

sitting quietly in my closet?

Jean Varda ~ Chico, California

Recipe for Comfort

Cinnamon nutmeg ginger
cardamon, one cup of whole milk
a half teaspoon of vanilla
one teaspoon of honey.
Warm in saucepan for three minutes
curl up on a sofa with a soft blanket,
and a book of poems.
Open the window two inches to
listen to the rain and wind,
breathe in breathe out.
Rub lavender lotion on your feet.
Recite one poem out loud slowly.
Count each breath till you get
to one hundred.
Rock in the rocking chair
then crawl into bed with your cat
soft as velvet.

Mariana Warner ~ Asheville, North Carolina

This bluebird, disguised. . .
(untitled haiku chain)

This bluebird, disguised
as a leaf on an almost-bare
maple tree branch, leaks

his location, bursts
into song, giving away
his sole exalted

perch. Preening, he fans
one wing, blue as the brightest
cerulean sky.

Revealing his place
to the birder far below,
he then flies away

like a dream gone by
on a wing and a prayer
by a heavenly choir.

Tanya Whitney ~ Sorrento, Louisiana

Descent of the Leaves

The temperatures are quickly cooling
as the season moves into autumn.
It is an impending change of seasons
much like in the evolution of our lives.

As young children, the falling leaves
were a haven for us, a place of fun.
Jumping in and out, then burying
one another in crisp, crackling covers.

As every season of life approached,
the tumbling leaves became drudgery.
We became youngsters on the threshold
of adulthood, shrouded in hormones.

We cursed the time spent raking and
disposing of those same dying leaves.
Never again, would the joy that we once
shared as children prevail in our lives.

In the season of our silvered twilight,
the descent of leaves brings new meaning.
They represent the days that have passed
never to be recovered or recaptured.

For they are gradually dying as we are
though they bring renewal to the land.
Laying a cover of warmth upon the earth,
our joy now is only in the changing colors.

One day they will drape our silent graves
as we eternally sleep in their warm cocoon.
So rejoice in the comfort of the falling leaves
for they are the kaleidoscope of our lives.

Eva Willis ~ Phoenix, Arizona

Finding Art

Art is not straightening
the unevenness of nature.
It is embracing it and
sharing it in words or
pictures. Can you describe
daybreak so perfectly that
a blind man can see it?
Can you paint or draw so
well as to place me
somewhere I am not and
may never have been?

I find art in nature. Silken
strands of spider web
sparkle with recent rain
drops that cling and quiver.
The morning sun when it
starts to explore my bedroom
as I watch it come alive. That
same sun peeking through the
glass blocks in my bathroom
to shine dancing light under
a wooden leaping dolphin above
my jacuzzi tub. Masterpiece
Theatre dramas on Sunday
nights where hazy, diffused light
filters through old windows
between white lace curtains
into rooms filled with cosmic
dust on books, cluttered desks,
and antique wing-back chairs.

ARIZONA STATE POETRY SOCIETY
2023 Board of Directors

ELECTED EXECUTIVE BOARD

President. . . . . Katie Zale
Vice President. . . . . .Ron Zack
Secretary. . . . . .Johnny Chavez/David Navarro
Communications Director. . . . . Renee Palting
Treasurer/Membership. . . . . .Kris Perry

APPOINTED BOARD OFFICERS - BRANCH PRESIDENTS

East Valley Poets President. . . . . Jim Platt
Scottsdale Mustang Poets President. . . . . CChristy White
Tucson Poetry Society President. .Elaine Powers

APPOINTED BOARD CHAIRPEOPLE

Annual Conference. . . . . Jim Platt
Annual Contest. . . . . CChristy White
Member Contests. . . . . Dianne Brown
Youth Contest . . . . CChristy White
Program Development. . . . . .Alan Perry
Sandcutters Co-Editors. . . . . .Kris Perry / CChristy White

We invite you to visit the ASPS website to learn more about our organi-zation, to order past issues of *Sandcutters*, and/or to join our growing or-ganization so you can participate in everything we have to offer, includ-ing our Branch zoom meetings.

https://azpoetry.net/

ASPS PRESIDENTS

1966-67	Maybelle Lyon
1968-71	Waunetta Hackleman
1972-73	Jean Humphrey Chaillie
1974	Alfarata Hansel
1975	Nat Zausner
1976	Margaret Mary Eitzen
1977	Dr. Raymond Emery
1978	Jane Spain
1979	Florence Otter
1980	Frank Rodocker
1981-82	Dorothy Lykes
1983	Edythe Bregnard
1984	Edward Haehl
1985-86	Jack Evans
1987-88	Olive Merchant
1989	Jack Evans
1990	Genevieve Sargent
1991	Lois Faram
1992-94	Priscilla White
1995	Robert Nagle
1996-97	Bob Nelson
1998-99	Jim Groundwater
200-01	Karen Odle
2002-03	Dorothy Zahner
2004	Ernest R. Griffith
2005-06	Kristen Ann Morton
2007	Jose Garcia
2008-09	Artiste-Te (Earl Teteak)
2010-15	CChristy White
2016-17	Carol Hogan
2018-22	CChristy White
2023-	Katie Zale

AUTHOR INDEX

AUTHOR INDEX

AUTHOR INDEX

AUTHOR INDEX

Back Cover: Black Silky Flycatcher
Artist: Kim Sosin

Made in the USA
Las Vegas, NV
20 December 2023